Commuter Marriage

LIVING TOGETHER, APART

Fairlee E. Winfield

Illustrations by Louise Waller

New York   Columbia University Press   1985

Printed in the United States of America

Columbia University Press
New York   Guildford, Surrey

Library of Congress Cataloging in Publication Data

Winfield, Fairlee E.
  Commuter Marriage.

  Bibliography: p.
  Includes index.
  1. Marriage—United States.   2. Married people—
Employment—United States.   3. Married people—
United States—Social conditions.   I. Title.
HQ734.W7645   1985   306.8'1   84-17528
ISBN 0-231-05948-5 (alk. paper)

Clothbound editions of Columbia University Press books are Smyth-sewn and
printed on permanent and durable acid-free paper.

To my husband for making life a joy.
To National Public Radio for making miles fly by.

Contents

Acknowledgments

This book would not have been possible without the help of commuter husbands and wives who took time to share information with me about their unusual lifestyle. They did so with the understanding that their anonymity would be respected, and so names and some identifying details have been changed throughout this book.

I want to thank Myra Dinnerstein at the Southwest Institute for Research on Women (SIROW) for help and suggestions in obtaining information from business and union sources.

Janice Blood, Director of Public Information at 9 to 5, the National Association of Office Workers, in Boston provided me with some interesting anecdotes on "pink collar" women and the clerical commuters. She allowed me to see how the interests of these workers are related to those of women in higher economic levels, and how the recent economic crisis has affected these women, who found themselves suddenly the major "breadwinner" of the family.

I am indebted to Juliet Carroll, Constance Carroll, Karen Onufrock, and Paula Barnes, who provided contacts with commuters in all parts of the United States and encouraged them to respond to the questionnaire.

I am grateful to Martha Blue, who pointed out information on the legal aspects of the marriage contract, and to the Bureau of Business and Economic Research at Northern Arizona

University, College of Business Administration, which provided me with help in producing and mailing my questionnaire and with postage for facilitating responses. Jackie Begay did a fine job of transcribing the manuscript on the word processor at the bureau.

Louise Waller's illustrations vividly depict the joys and woes of the commuter lifestyle. I am profoundly grateful for her inspired creativity.

Finally, the book is possible only because of the unfailing support of my husband, Hal Blankenship, who is a commuter spouse and my best friend.

I am grateful for permission to quote excerpts from the following:

P. Berger and H. Keller, "Marriage and the Construction of Reality." *Diogenes*, (1964). 64:1–23. Copyright © 1964 by *Diogenes*.

Philip Blumstein and Pepper Schwartz, *American Couples: Money, Work, Sex*. New York: William Morrow, 1983. Copyright © 1983 by William Morrow.

William Borders, "Away-on-Work Husbands and Marital Strains." *New York Times*, November 10, 1980. Copyright © 1980 by The New York Times Company.

Linda Cecere, "The Loneliness of the Long-Distance Marriage." *Working Woman* (October 1983), pp. 136–39. Copyright © 1983 by Hal Publications.

Mary Crawford, "Two Careers, Three Kids, and Her 2,000 Mile Commute." *Ms.* (August 1979), pp. 76–78. Copyright © 1979 by Hal Publications.

W. Randolph Flynn and Judith U. Litzsinger, "Careers Without Conflict." *Personnel Administrator* (July 1981), p. 81. Copyright © 1981 by The American Society for Personnel Administration.

Dick Friedman, "Where His Career Leads Would You Follow?" *Working Woman* (June 1981), pp. 15–18. Copyright © 1981 by Hal Publications.

Liz Roman Gallese, "Moving Experiences: Women Managers Say Job Transfers Present a Growing Dilemma." *Wall Street Journal* (May 4, 1978), p. 1. Copyright © 1983 by Dow Jones & Company, Inc. All rights reserved.

Judy Gaylin, "How Supermoms Can Cope." *Family Weekly* (October 9, 1983), p. 19. Copyright © 1983 by *Family Weekly*.

George Getschow, "A Tale of Two Cities Has an Unhappy End for Some Executives." *Wall Street Journal* (February 1, 1980), p. 1. Copyright © 1980 by Dow Jones and Company, Inc. All rights reserved.

Evelyn Goodrick, "Making a Commuter Marriage Work." *McCall's* (July 1980), p. 68. Copyright © 1980 by *McCall's*.

Earl C. Gottschalk, "Trendy Dwellings: The Affordable' Home Turns Out to Be Tiny and Not Really Cheap." *Wall Street Journal* (December 7, 1983), p. 1. Copyright © 1983 by Dow Jones & Company, Inc. All rights reserved.

Harriet Engel Gross, "Dual-Career Couples Who Live Apart: Two Types." *Journal of Marriage and the Family* (August 1980), pp. 567–76. Copyright © 1980 by the National Council on Family Relations.

Shere Hite, *The Hite Report*. New York: Macmillan, 1976. Copyright © 1976 by Shere Hite.

Patricia Hogan, "Career Women and Changing Lifestyles." *Executive Female* (July–August 1980), pp. 34–38. Copyright © 1980 by *The Executive Female* magazine, publication of the National Association for Female Executives.

Bill Hunter, "On the Job Relocation." *Working Woman* (February 1982), pp. 16–18. Copyright © 1982 by Hal Publications.

Janice Kaplan, "He/She." *Self* (March 1979), pp. 38–41. Copyright © 1979 by The Condé Nast Publications.

Betty Frankle Kirschner and Laurel Richardson Walum, "Two-Location Families." *Alternative Lifestyles* (November 1978), pp. 513–26. Copyright © 1978 by Human Sciences Press.

Monica Langley, "Some U.S. Jobs Turn Strong Marriages into Weekend Ones." *Wall Street Journal* (August 18, 1981), p. 1. Copyright © 1981 by Dow Jones & Company, Inc. All rights reserved.

John Leo, "Marital Tales of Two Cities." *Time* (January 25, 1982), pp. 83–84. Copyright © 1982 by Time Inc.

Larry McMurty, "Silent Nights, Empty Days: Leaving Loneliness Behind." *Family Weekly* (December 11, 1983), p. 4. Copyright © 1983 by *Family Weekly*.

Mary F. Maples, "Dual Career Marriages: Elements for Potential Success." *The Personnel and Guidance Journal* (September 1981), pp. 19–23. Copyright © 1981 by AACD (American Association for Counseling and Development). No further reproduction authorized without permission of AACD.

Cathleen E. Maynard and Robert A. Zawacki, "Organizations Must Meet This Challange: Is Yours Ready?" *Personnel Journal* (July 1979), pp. 469–72. Copyright © July 1979 by *Personnel Journal*.

William C. Nichols, "Long-Distance Marriage." *Parents Magazine* (October 1978), p. 54. Copyright © 1978 by Parents Magazine Enterprises.

Patricia O'Toole, "The Unhappy Lot of the Academic Couple with Two Careers and One Job." *The Chronicle of Higher Education* (September 14, 1983), p. 64. Copyright © 1977 by *The Chronicle of Higher Education*.

Rhonda Rapoport, Robert N. Rapoport, and Ziona Strelitz with Stephen Kew, *Fathers, Mothers, and Society*. New York: Basic Books, 1977. Copyright © 1977 by Basic Books.

Sheila Rule, "Long-Distance Marriage on the Rise," *New York Times* (October 31, 1977), p. 33. Copyright © 1977 by The New York Times Company.

Barbara Toman, "Parenthood and Career Overtax Some Women Despite Best Intentions." *Wall Street Journal* (September 7, 1983), p. 1. Copyright © 1983 by Dow Jones & Company, Inc. All rights reserved.

"Twenty at the Top." *Savvy* (April 1983), pp. 38–47. Copyright © 1983 by SAVVY Magazine Inc., SAVVY Co.

Introduction

"Why is it always assumed that a woman's work is the lesser job and that she must always bend?" said Kathy. She was standing by the gray filing cabinet with the sign-in sheet taped to its side. It was barely 8:00 A.M., and the usual hectic scramble in the office technology lab at Yavapai Community College in Flagstaff had not yet reached its peak.

"You know," she continued, "I played the role of trailing spouse until Ruthy started school and I became an instructor here, but now Ed and I have weighed the alternatives and we've decided to opt for a new lifestyle. I guess you could say it's my turn."

It wasn't so long ago that married couples with two careers were considered exceptional. Now that pattern is undergoing change. Kathy and Ed are happily married, but living apart. And they are not unique.

"I'm not going this weekend, Liz. I'm too tired and things are piling up. Ruthy has a school program and I've arranged for delivery of the firewood. I hate it, but Ed is just going to do without the tools he wanted me to bring up to Prescott."

"I'm leaving at three," Liz answered, "as soon as I get rid of the students' questions on their projects. If the traffic's not bad, I'll be in Tucson by 8:30 tonight."

"How long have you been commuting anyway? I thought Prescott was a long drive, but Tucson—every week!"

"Six months now, and before that, the three months while Bob was in Page," replied Liz.

A slim woman wearing an Evan-Picone tweed suit, about 42, had joined the group. "Why don't you two get your husbands to do the commuting? Allen drives from Phoenix every weekend. With teenagers around there's no way I could drive all the time. I'm hoping that the job in Maricopa County comes through. Then we'll all move to Phoenix, but I'm *not* going until I have a good government position down there and until I sell the house up here." Meg, who had spoken, was a supervisor in the Coconino County Court offices.

"I don't know Meg, I've gotten so I enjoy the drive to Tucson. I have five hours alone to collect my wits, listen to jazz, blue-grass, and 'All Things Considered,' or to just relax and think without interruptions. Besides, Tucson is a real city; I love it— great restaurants, fantastic shopping, first-run movies. It's a honeymoon every week. It's a relief to get out of this snow and ice, and then I come back on Monday morning and get into the job for four days."

"I have to admit that Ed and I get along better now that he's in Prescott. Our marriage seems better. It was always good, but now we do less haggling and hassling of one another. There's not a lot of time for it, just for the good things. It's my mom and dad who don't like the idea," said Kathy. "Is Bill still in Marble Canyon?" she asked a new arrival.

"Yes, our biggest problem is time, and then the travel and phone calls are getting expensive. We're now writing letters, but it looks like we'll continue commuting until his business is established."

A woman at the Commodore Pet near the end of the row of word processors turned her swivel chair and joined the commuters by the filing cabinets. "I've been offered a job in Phoenix."

"Great!"

"Congratulations!"

"Hope the salary's good!"

"It is, but my husband's working at Walgreen's here in Flag."

"Are you going to take the Phoenix job?"

"We've talked a lot about it and finally decided that we can't afford not to. The only offer I've had here was from that lawyer's office that wanted to pay me $3.75 an hour with no career ladder. I'm going to Phoenix, Mike will stay here, and we'll commute."

It was in just this way that this book got started. Among the small group of women there at Yavapai that early spring morning, half of them were living a new lifestyle that is becoming known as "commuter marriage." During the three years of my marriage, I had been a commuter for eighteen months. Nevertheless, I found it surprising that there were so many of us. Suddenly, everyone seemed to be doing it. But not everyone was successful. The marriage of a department chairperson whose wife was commuting by air from an East Coast college had just ended in divorce.

Many academic couples, theater people, politicians, and journalists commuted; but the women at Yavapai were from a different group—the group in which wives traditionally give up jobs to follow husbands whose careers take precedence. I began to ask some questions:

1. Who are the married commuters anyway?
2. Why do they choose this lifestyle?
3. What makes a commuter marriage work?
4. How do these couples resolve the small questions such as who will mop the kitchen floor in which house, or who will make the dental checkup appointments and in which location?
5. How do these couples resolve the large questions such as whose career comes first, or how will the extra money from two careers be spent?
6. What was the response of business, government, family, friends, and social groups to this brand new social structure that everyone was calling "commuter marriage"?

The intention of this book is to allow commuter couples, or those considering a commuter relationship, to get acquainted with and to share their experiences and feelings. It will talk about dual-household marriage as an option and include facts about what's good and bad about commuting. It will let you understand what commuting does to a marriage, to children, to the commuters themselves. Although reading the book can't guarantee success at commuter marriage, it will give a lot of information on how other people have been successful. The book will explore one of the major developments affecting dual-earner couples—long-distance marriage.

The information contained in this book is gathered from several sources. First, in-depth interviews were conducted with 59 spouses in commuter marriages. Twelve of these interviews included both husband and wife. Second, 100 questionnaires were mailed to commuter couples in all parts of the United States. Replies were anonymous. The questions asked were open ended; that is, the person replying answered with a statement rather than merely circling an answer. Finally, interviews were conducted with business organizations such as International Business Machines and General Dynamics, and with unions such as the National Association of Working Women, 9 to 5. In addition to the primary information obtained from these sources the book also uses biographical studies and other information on two-location families included in 52 articles published between 1977 and 1984 in academic journals, popular magazines, newspapers, news magazines, and business media. These articles include information from approximately 300 commuter couples.

The information obtained from the sources above suggests that there is no particular need to distinguish between middle-class and working-class commuter marriages. Focus will be on commuter couples as a whole new social structure rather than on a particular social class, since the problems and pleasures are much the same. When we look at activities, interests, and opinions of commuter couples, all seem to think very much the same. Differences, if any, are less related to psychographics than they are to economics. Two residences are an economic burden, even with two salaries to partially compensate. In cases where money makes a difference, the difference will be explored.

"Temporary" commuting, just like the temporary job, becomes permanent as the traditional "someday we'll get together" two-city couple commutes a little longer and becomes less traditional. All research and statistics suggest that dual-residence marriage is increasing. As women climb the job ladder, the philosophy of "Whither thou goest, I will go" is being forgotten.

Commuter Marriage

Chapter One
"Whither Thou Goest . . . Thou Goest"
The New Lifestyle

Strictly speaking, commuter marriage is illegal. As of 1983 only five states had laws saying a married person could establish his or her own domicile. Lenore Weitzman in her book *The Marriage Contract* (1981) looks at marriage as a social, legal entity and states what has been suspected for a long time. It is indeed the husband's right to say where the couple shall live. This began with common law that made the husband head-of-household and gave him the authority to choose the marital abode. The wife was obliged to follow him wherever he went and to live under whatever circumstances he chose. Three outmoded assumptions underlie the domicile law: (1) the husband's work determines the family residence because the woman is solely responsible for domestic services; (2) husbands alone are responsible for family support; and (3) all families are single-career.

As outmoded as these assumptions may be, they are ingrained in the cultural system because they have been derived from laws and legal constraints that influence our most intimate relationships. The common law heritage of legal marriage established the rights and responsibilities of husbands and wives, and provided sanctions against those who did not comply. "The reality of law is to be found not in legal tomes alone but in the social definitions of ordinary people," says Weitzman.

People assume that a family consists of two opposite-sex adults living in the same household. Social scientists have always reinforced this definition. D. M. Schneider (1978:33) emphasized the residence requirements in his book *American Kinship* when he stated: "The family to be a family, must live together." If any other condition prevails, the family is broken. The Bureau of the Census defines a married couple as "a husband and wife enumerated as members of the same household." Emphasis is always on living together, common residence, same household. How then can people in the eighties live apart and be married couples and families?

Historically there have been many circumstances under which members of the same family, husbands and wives, live in separate geographical locations. War has been a major reason for separation. Immigration is another. The salesman, the truck driver, the business executive, the harvester, the offshore oil worker, and the sheep shearer have always left the "little women" behind while they organized their lives around their work. The largest employer in the United States, the military, has traditionally demanded frequent separation of husband and wife.

But commuter marriage is emerging as a new pattern. In this case, it is the female partner and her career that are the important issue. The wife wishes to seize an opportunity to take a job away from "home" or wishes to remain in an attractive job in the present location when the spouse has an offer elsewhere. The commuting lifestyle is characterized by almost total compartmentalization of work and home life. During the days away from home, there is total involvement in work without interference from family demands, while weekends or times together are devoted totally to family. The choice for a commuting lifestyle is motivated entirely by career concerns.

When the domicile rule and the assumption of the husband's sole responsibility for family support prevailed, the situation was like the one described below. It is the story of Mike and Ann Finley told to *Personnel Administrator*, but it could easily be your story. Each has a job and the husband, Mike, is offered a better opportunity in a new location.

Mike and Ann Finley are a fairly typical couple. . . . They met and married while attending college. They also decided at that time they would become members of one of the fastest growing demographic units in the country—the dual career couple. After graduating with degrees in business administration, each found jobs with excellent career potential. Mike started his career as a personnel specialist with the local manufacturing division of a large national organization. Ann started as a management trainee with a rapidly growing bank operating in the same region.

Things progressed nicely for the next three years. Both had been cycled through several jobs as part of their development programs and both had received excellent promotions. They had each been singled out as fast-track candidates by their employers and their careers seemed assured. Then came the next promotion. Mike was offered the opportunity to move up to a management level position within the personnel department. The move up, as is typically the case, however, also required a move on. The new job was located in another city halfway across the state. After talking it over, they decided the offer was too good to turn down. Mike accepted the promotion, and Ann, after trying unsuccessfully for a transfer, resigned her position at the bank. She had sacrificed her career for his, and in her mind three years of hard work and progress were now in ruins. (Flynn and Litzsinger 1981:81)

Ann had adopted the role of "trailing spouse" that tradition demanded, and now she felt demeaned and downgraded because, although she had eventually found a job at another bank, it was considerably less prestigious than the position she gave up. Ann defined herself in a traditional way. The significant aspect of her relationship with Mike was the marriage, and she limited herself in a supportive wife role.

However, many women are defining themselves in such a way that the relative importance of career and marriage is changing. Today wives work because of financial necessity, because of career goals established before marriage, because of an increased demand for consumer goods and services, and most important because of self-fulfillment. Consequently, a wife may be unwilling to move with her husband, or she may be willing to move without him to pursue career goals. Commuter marriage comes not from failure but from success. It is a developing and possibly permanent solution for two-career couples because the individuals feel no need to choose between two very important aspects of their lives, a job and a relationship. They accept the job, and adjust the relationship.

But there is yet another important aspect to commuter marriage. Men too are defining themselves in a new way. They are rejecting the outmoded assumption that they alone are responsible for family support, and rejecting the notion that only a woman should handle child care and domestic services. Men today expect their wives to work. The dual-career family is rapidly becoming the norm. Men today are also beginning to assume a much larger role in parenting and home life as a part of their self-fulfillment. Their marginal position in the home is disappearing. Consequently, men in commuter families more readily accept the major parenting and domestic tasks. They too are motivated by career concerns—not necessarily one career, but the careers of both spouses.

Commuter marriage, then, is a situation in which a couple decides to live together, apart. It is basically a female-determined relationship, as opposed to the traditional male-determined traveling salesman situation.

Both a job *and* an intimate relationship are highly important. Commuter marriage is a new social structure for which there are no rules and few norms. Friends and family of commuter couples consider the arrangement downright exotic. One woman who for career development established a commuter marriage reported that her new colleagues persisted in talking about her "ex-husband." She spent three months in explanations before they stopped talking about the divorce.

Because the Census Bureau defines a married couple as "same household," there is no possible way to determine accurately the incidence of dual-residence marriage. What *Alternative Lifestyles* (Kirschner and Walum 1978) called the "married-single" doesn't seem to exist. But *Time* in January 1982 stated, "There are at least 700,000 commuter couples according to some estimates" (Leo 1982:83). Everything suggests that the number of such marriages is increasing as women climb the job ladder and cast aside the "Whither thou goest, I will go" philosophy. The increase may also be related to the shift in attitude among males that finds husbands now welcoming the additional income from their wives' jobs. As the so-called acquisitive generation comes of age, double income seems a middle-class necessity. Sixty percent of all families with an income of $20,000 or more are dual-earner couples. In 1979, 2.6 million women were employed in managerial and administrative jobs in private industry and government.

Culturally there still remains a distinction between dual-career and dual-occupation couples. Mary Maples (1981:6) in the *Personnel and Guidance Journal* says, "Many, if not most, women who are married and working are doing so more out of necessity than of desire." These women are said to be the basis for designation of the category "dual-occupation." Maples proposes that these working wives lack commitment to their work roles, have little preparation, experience, or training for work, and don't generally take a great deal of personal or professional pride in their work. If the distinction exists, it should be easier to visualize by looking at two profiles of real couples to see how it would work. The first story was told in *Colorado Woman* (Hagen 1980:45), the second in a personal interview.

A Typical Dual-Career Couple
Yvonne and Stan. Yvonne returned to school in the late sixties when her four children were teenagers and she was in her 40s. She and her husband Stan, who is a deputy district attorney in Portland, Oregon, discussed the possibility that after she finished her studies at Portland State University they might be separated. In 1973 Yvonne received her Ph.D. in Environmental Sciences and Resources. While she was working on her Ph.D., the couple had a taste of living apart. She worked as a volunteer for the Idaho and Oregon Game and Fish departments during the summers to gain experience. Upon receiving her doctorate Yvonne went to work for the Army Corps of Engineers on habitation and evaluation studies. In 1978, she moved to Fort Collins, Colorado, where she is director of Habitation Evaluation Procedures. She supervises a team of fifteen engaged in putting out

a handbook for fish and wildlife personnel on life requisites. When her story was the subject of a *Colorado Woman* article in 1980, Stan was living in Portland, Oregon, with their daughter (the other three children had graduated from college), and the couple was commuting on alternate weekends between Fort Collins, Colorado, and Portland, Oregon. Yvonne and Stan are a typical dual-career commuting couple.

A Typical Dual-Occupation Couple

Marilyn and Fred. Marilyn returned to work in a clerical position while her three children were all under 12 years old. The two boys had a series of illnesses that had required hospitalization, and the family was $3,000 in debt in spite of the medical insurance that Fred had with the Milwaukee brewery where he was a unionized, skilled blue-collar worker. Marilyn and Fred decided that she would help him only until the bills were paid off and would then return to being a full-time housewife. But there was trouble in earmarking the money for the medical bills. Sometimes car payments, licenses, and other things came due all at once. Marilyn felt she could use her time for household tasks better if she had a microwave oven, and then Fred needed a new outboard for the Whaler. Two years passed, and the insurance company where Marilyn worked began to move into office automation. Marilyn began training as a word processing operator and found she not only liked the work, she was very good at it. She began taking introductory night courses in data and information processing at a community college. Three years later she was manager of word processing, in charge of twenty employees in the company's information processing center. Office technology was becoming an important aspect of business, and although Marilyn had no college diploma, she knew office technology and had eight years of experience in a rapidly expanding field. Her employers discovered that she was talented at understanding the organization's changing paperwork needs and the equipment required to handle those needs. She was promoted to the position of systems analyst for the ten Wisconsin offices of Nichols Insurance Company in 1982. Meanwhile, Fred had also received some promotions. He became section supervisor and was a leader in the union. Marilyn and Fred often discussed her quitting and returning to being a full-time housewife (she still continued to do most of the household chores when she was not traveling for the company), but she was unwilling now to forfeit her hard-to-come-by job. Marilyn likes her central position in the company where her decisions and advice on equipment needs are respected. Both Fred and Marilyn have grown used to the lifestyle affordable with two incomes, and Fred is now beginning to encourage Marilyn to continue being a "working wife." They agree that he is the "breadwinner," but is she merely a "cakewinner"?

The Vanishing Occupation/Career Distinction

The dual-occupation, dual-career distinction would say that the first couple, Yvonne and Stan, are dual-career while Marilyn and Fred are dual-occupation, since Marilyn began work more out of necessity than out of desire. However, this distinction is extremely hard to maintain when we look at the profile of Marilyn and Fred. First, to be a "working wife" rather than a "career woman" Marilyn must lack commitment to her work. But Marilyn *is* committed to her position, so much so that she refuses to give it up now that the family's financial difficulty has been resolved. She is also committed to her income, which has allowed the family to acquire the luxury items they have grown to appreciate. Second, if Marilyn is in an "occupation" rather than a "career," she should have little preparation, experience, or training for the work. Although Marilyn doesn't have the Ph.D. degree Yvonne has, she has had over ten years of experience with her company. She has grown with the company, and she has continued technical training on her own in order to keep up with the developments in her field. Finally, a working wife is said to lack personal and professional pride in her work. But Marilyn's continued training and her central position of trust with the company demonstrate her professionalism.

Clearly, the chasm between the two types of couples is no longer a chasm. As more women enter the work force and remain there longer, we may be looking at merely a crack in the sidewalk. It is interesting to note that in the first place the distinction between the two types of couples is made upon the basis of the *wife's* attitude toward work. Because of the head-of-household assumption in the unwritten marriage contract, men are not allowed an ambivalent attitude toward work. They simply must do it. There are probably many men who would prefer not to work, yet this is not considered the basis on which to form a socially distinct category. Many future dual-career couples are represented initially in the dual-occupation or working-couple group, and the distinction will certainly have disappeared by 1990. The *Monthly Labor Review* predicts that by that time, the female participation rate in the labor force will reach 60 percent; whereas in 1967, the rate for women aged 16 or older was merely 41 percent (Grossman 1981:60).

Meanwhile, the male participation rate is expected to drop somewhat. This says that fewer men may be working and that women are going to work in ever-increasing numbers, and most of them will be married. One estimate today indicates that 48 percent of all American wives are now employed or looking for work. More important, women are no longer "helpmates" but are making significant inroads into traditional male bastions as more and more women demand equality in employment and careers that are both challenging and satisfying. The whole structure of the job market for both men and women is undergoing significant and rapid change, and the whole structure of marital relationships is also undergoing significant and rapid change. The temporary job to help out becomes a permanent career. The commuting done on a temporary basis until two jobs are located in the same geographic area becomes a challenging and satisfying means of maintaining both an intimate relationship and a career. Ann Finley chose career sacrifice. The willingness to do this, however, is going to change as new job opportunities unfold, and as couples and employers learn more about how it is possible to sustain a long-distance relationship.

Whither Thou Goest . . .

Another woman who chose career sacrfice is Nancy Richardson. Nancy and Bob were in their late 40s when the company where he had worked for twenty-two years felt compelled to transfer him to Pittsburgh because he was working in specialized research that could be done better there. Nancy had a family and a supervisory nursing job for which she had worked very hard. She had gained the respect and friendship of all her fellow workers in the Ohio town where the couple had lived for years. Nancy at first refused to move. She resisted for three years, and during this period Bob commuted each weekend. Bob says that during this time "divorce was discussed many times, seriously." The marriage was severely strained, and Nancy finally agreed to move. The Richardson's two college-age sons had also become concerned. They didn't like the friction between their parents, and they didn't want them to get a divorce. Nancy moved—but Nancy is not happy living in Pittsburgh without her friends and her career position. She is working as a nurse, but the job is in another speciality, and not her first choice. It was only with the encouragement of professional relocation counseling that Nancy was finally convinced to move.

The problem here is that all efforts were directed at getting Nancy to follow Bill, to become the trailing spouse required by the unwritten marriage contract. She had to go along with the traditional "whither thou goest" philosophy (which, incidentally, had nothing at all to do with husbands and wives in the biblical version but with two women, Ruth and Naomi). Nor was Bill encouraged to seek other solutions. His employers, the couple's children, the relocation counselor all turned their efforts toward protecting Bill's career and preserving the traditional single-career two-person concept. While the couple was commuting the pressures of the long-distance living plan were exaggerated by the social expectation that Nancy should indeed relocate and should follow Bill. The pressure made Bill feel less masculine if Nancy didn't tag along. For Bill the salient aspect of his relationship with Nancy is his work. He defines himself in terms of the traditional marriage contract role of primary breadwinner and Nancy in the traditional role of supplying supportive domestic services. Few options are then open, and the barriers to a successful commuter marriage are all firmly in place. These barriers make up a series of rigid *you're not spozed tos* for both the husband and the wife.

Women Aren't Spozed To:	*Men Aren't Spozed To:*
live apart from husband	allow a wife to decide where to live
live apart from children	take care of children
seek vertical mobility	ignore vertical mobility
earn more than husband	earn less than wife
be boss	be supportive
be competitive	be emotional
be ambitious	be unambitious
be objective	be sensitive

Commuter marriage, like any relationship, can indeed be stressful, but it is a separation by choice. And with a little knowledge, with a new response from employers, with a positive response from friends and relatives, and with the support of social groups, it can succeed. It is successful right now for thousands of couples. The lifestyle should be seen as one way to integrate and manage a career and family life. Commuting has its stresses, but it also has its pleasures.

Chapter Two

"For Better or for Worse . . . in Sickness and in Health"

Psychic Stresses and Psychic Pleasures

I think it's crazy. Couples with divergent careers can, with some effort, if they consider the relationship important enough, look for ways to deal with both careers. The idea of living apart in separate cities for more than just a temporary period is a decision for career and not for marriage. Absence does not make the heart grow fonder.

Marriage and Family Consultation Center, Houston
(Van Hulsteyn 1978)

Over the long term, there are very few couples who can pull off a commuting arrangement and manage to have anything left in the usual context called marriage. . . . A crucial ingredient in marriage is shared experience, if these experiences are decreased beyond some lower limit, the relationship is fragmented.

Counseling Service, Harvard Business School
(*Business Week* 1978)

Amid these dire predictions of disaster, more than 700,000 people are putting it on the line and trying it anyway. They say, "What's implicit in our living arrangements is that our particular positions are more important to us than each other at this point . . . maybe you consider that a miserable statement; we don't."

Who are the married commuters anyway? What are the psychographics of commuting? What motivates the commuters to defy convention? Is it possible to categorize them? We could look at the amount of money they make. We could look at their educational levels. We could look at the types of jobs they hold. We could look at their age, number of children, whether or not they own their own home, or rather homes. All these are important, and they contribute to the psychic stresses and psychic pleasures of commuting families. But in the long run we would find that there is an enormously broad range of answers.

Commuters come from all economic levels, hold all sorts of jobs. They have from none to eight or even ten children. They are from all educational levels, and all age levels. Since they always have two homes, there are patterns of rent-rent, own-own, rent-own, own-rent, with townhouses, condos, suburban single-family homes, sharing with parents or family, hotel rooms, apartments, duplexes, high-rises, and even houseboats involved. Separations also run a continuum from several days apart each week to cross-country relationships where encounters are far more rare. Because there is such a broad range, instead of going into details, it is more interesting to look at ideas commuters seem to have in common, to try and find out more about how they think, their values, activities, interests, and opinions. A good way to start is to look at four common circumstances in which commuter marriages occur. While reading, keep in mind that all the two-location couples have two major typifying characteristics. First, they are totally committed to their intimate relationship with each other, and second, they are totally committed to their careers.

Four Circumstances of Commuter Marriage

The Young Professionals

Janet and George married when they were still in graduate school. They were both seeking advanced degrees in plant pathology. With so much common interest, they felt ideally suited to each other. Weekends were spent hiking in the area and gathering and preserving specimens. They both enjoyed camping, and in the summers they had an enormous vegetable garden where they grew most of the food they needed for the year. Both were vegetarians and "natural food freaks." There was never a question about one of them giving up a career if they couldn't find positions in the same location. Janet was to finish her degree a year before George, and she began job-hunting in the Massachusetts university town where George would be staying to complete his work in botany. About that time, however, she received an offer from a New York state university to be in charge of their Plant Pathology Extension Service Program. It was an offer Janet couldn't turn down. It would have been impossible to alter either partner's career goals; so after a discussion and a balance-sheet approach, they decided to alter their relationship. They both needed experience before they could achieve their long-range goal of having their own consulting business.

Janet moved to New York and they arranged a commuter relationship. At first they tried to get together each weekend, but it soon became obvious that with a graduate thesis to write for George and a new, demanding job for Janet, the driving time and fatigue would be impossible to manage. They switched to every other week and to special long times together on holidays. The year passed and George graduated, but there was no position for him in the town where Janet was working. George did find a position in New York, working with diseases of apple trees in a town about a three-hour drive away from Janet. They both have rented apartments in the towns where they live and can frequently get together not only for weekends but during the week when their schedules aren't too heavy. They're now considering buying a house in a small town that is halfway between their two work locations. Whose career comes first? Janet replies, "Mine. I graduated and became employed first. This may change later, for reasons of fair play *only!* Or for reasons of job preference elsewhere on my part." George says, "Janet's career comes first at the moment . . . because her position is guaranteed while mine is as yet temporary. We have hopeful plans for an eventual joint business and for being together permanently sometime soon."

The Relocatees

For nineteen years, Sharon followed her husband, Jack, from one part of the country to another while he pursued his career as a physician who teaches and does research. Sharon remembers that it was always "What's best for Jack?" or "What's best for the family?" But last year Sharon joined the growing ranks of women who no longer automatically accommodate their own lives and careers to their husbands' needs. When Jack took a position at a university in California, Sharon stopped moving. She simply refused to go. She explained, "I decided it was time to do what was best for *me!*" The best meant remaining in New York City, where as a result of years of volunteer work for the League of Women Voters, she had been offered a job in the political unit of a network news operation. Although Sharon had been a laboratory assistant (that's how she met Jack), she had not worked for seventeen years while her children were growing up. She felt that the opportunity to start a new, meaningful career at 42 was too important to ignore.

"We decided that Jack would go to the Coast alone, and I would stay here with the kids—and my job. We knew that our marriage was strong enough to endure the separation—Jack comes home once every month for about a week at a time—and that my potential career was important enough to make sacrifices for. Both my consciousness and his had been raised sufficiently to appreciate my needs." Sharon believes that if she had not taken the position, there might never have been another offer (Delatiner 1981:87).

The Well-Established

The well-established are those couples who both have important and possibly even prestigious careers in different cities when they wed, but they choose to continue their two-city lifestyle. Frequently the well-established are also "well-heeled," famous, and highly visible. And this makes for a colorful existence.

The story of one of these couples was described in *Time* in January 1982. It is the story of Kaity Tong, 32, and Bob Long, 37. She is a newscaster at WABC-TV in New York City, and he is an independent TV producer-director in Los Angeles. In 1982, Kaity and Bob had been a couple for eight years and a married couple for four years; yet they never lived together in the same town or the same house. As a rookie at *Eyewitness News*, Kaity was on seven days a week; so Bob flew to New York to spend two weeks with her every month. At that time the rest of the marriage was conducted by telephone. They admit to talking six or seven times a day, and their phone bills averaged $800 per month. Bob said he would "tuck her in at night and wake her up in the morning by phone." The couple used various paging and answering services to maintain accessibility. "There is nothing good about separation, but we refuse to let it be an obstacle. She thinks I'm cute and I'm in love with her. The rest is mechanics" (Leo 1982:83).

The Economically Motivated

The fourth situation may be the most precarious, but it is also the one that may be expanding most rapidly as dual-occupation couples become dual-career couples and as people seek a higher standard of living. The assumption that the "working wife" is a supplementary wage earner is no longer valid. The recent economic situation has made this most evident. The National Association of Working Women, 9 to 5, notes that during the layoffs of the recent economic crisis when so many blue collar husbands suddenly became unemployed, clerical women workers realized for the first time that although they were highly skilled full-time workers, they were unable to support their husbands and families. Janice Blood, public relations director for 9 to 5, suggests that this is creating a trend toward unionization and demands for higher wages. Currently, skilled clerical employees receive lower wages than unskilled laborers. It has become clear to these women that their jobs provide more than supplementary income; their income is essential.

Charles and Myra are a good example. They had been married for twelve years. Charles was a skilled carpenter who

found himself unemployed in 1982 when the construction industry was severely depressed in the Southwest. Charles and Myra
were both 32. Myra had gone back into the work force in a
secretarial position when Jimmy, their 9-year-old, started school.
They owned a three-bedroom, one-story frame house in a very
nice neighborhood of the small city in which they lived. In fact,
Myra had been raised in the house. Her dad and her uncle built
it in 1950, and Myra's parents sold the house to the couple in
1974 at a highly advantageous interest rate. They had a "nice
little red Honda Accord . . . with a lot of parking lot dents." Myra
had been working with her company for three years and was
beginning to feel a part of the organization. The company liked
Myra and her work. They were giving her additional training in
information processing because they were expecting to auto-
mate their office systems within a few months. Charles helped
Myra around the house, did some needed repairs, and "a lot of
gardening and firewood cutting" while he was unemployed. The
months were dragging on, though, and the couple's finances,
even with their low mortgage payments, were getting to a crisis
state. Finally in August, Charles was offered a job in construction in Stanton, a city 160 miles from their home. The couple
considered the alternatives: they could all move to Stanton;
Myra could give up her job; they'd have to take Jimmy out of his
school; they would have to sell the house. Myra said "No, not
this time. I guess Jimmy would have been flexible enough to
make it, but I wasn't. I'm not sure whether it was the thought of
leaving the house or the thought of leaving my job that bothered me most. The truth was I couldn't leave either, and besides,
we weren't at that time very sure how long Charlie's job in
Stanton would last. It looked good, but who knows." The decision was finally made to commute. Myra says that they are now
looking at their careers "right down the middle." The job of
neither takes precedence. Myra even believes that "absence
does make the heart grow fonder." While away from Charles, she
says, she does more studying and working. "Getting together
again, feeling security, and not having to cope by myself during
our time together are the best parts of our commuter marriage."

Two Types of Commuter Families:
Adjusting and Established

Harriet Engle Gross, who looked at the rewards and strains of commuter marriage in 1980 by analyzing interviews with 43 spouses, believed there were two distinct types of couples engaged in these nontraditional marriages. The "adjusting" type was made up mainly of younger couples, while the "established" type was older. The distinction is helpful in identifying some common ways in which specific problems are experienced and dealt with. Before discussing these two types of commuters, Gross notes that it is helpful to look at the heritage of traditional marriage, because this is the vantage point from which all nontraditional marriage is seen by husbands and wives, even those who consciously reject standard marital roles. It is the only model for the marital relationship to which they can refer. Great pride is taken in the fact that two-city families "care about each other's careers," and great pride is taken that they are able to "pull off" the commuter lifestyle. But, as Gross (1980:569–70) notes, these statements acknowledge the disparity between their lifestyle and traditional marriage. The comparison is evident and causes psychic stress.

"More so than husbands in our culture," Gross notes (1980:570), "wives are programmed to think of marriage as an intimacy oasis—an emotionally close relationship that will be 'total.'" The powerful effect of this programming is seen in Myra's statement that the "feeling of security, and not having to cope by myself" are the best part of her reunions with her husband. In the face of all evidence to the contrary, even career-oriented women nurture dreams of Prince Charming, the dashing and gallant fellow who appears in a white Maserati and spirits them away to a rose-covered condo by the sea where they will live in bliss and cared-for comfort forever after. This is the fantasy world that is so lucrative for romance writers.

So, while the career-oriented commuter wife is experiencing the pressures of a professional career, there is simultaneously the loss of a heroic partner who had been expected to provide an emotional outlet as a sympathetic listener to the tales of the spunky heroine. Gross (1980:570) notes that in many of her interviews with commuters both husbands and wives remembered conversation in which the husband said to the wife, "You don't cry as much as you used to." But the statement came only after the initial career strains had somewhat abated.

Wives also recognize that responsibilities they expected to share or that their husbands would assume totally, they must now do themselves. One wife said, "I think it's a lot harder on me because not only have I had a house to take care of, but I had the wood to bring in, and the snow to shovel, and all the things that he usually does." Women are frequently pleased that they can deal with these experiences, but the added responsibility of household repairs is a burden. They know it shouldn't be a "big deal," but it is.

Men gain more in domestic services from traditional marriage than women, but the presumption that household maintenance will be their responsibility means that wives notice the extra chores. Some say, "It's a way of preparing for divorce or widowhood," while others save the chores for the weekend homecomings. A commuter husband lamented, "The worst thing about commuter marriage is the weekend—the lawn needs to be mowed, the car isn't running, the bathroom faucets are leaking, the swimming pool needs to be cleaned."

From the husbands' perspective, traditional marriage teaches them to expect intimacy too, but they are much less likely to express unhappiness over the loss of emotional closeness that living apart produces. Socialization doesn't encourage men to examine their feelings. They are much more likely to have learned that the rewards of work can take the place of interpersonal relationships. Men are apt to say, "We're each independent and do not rely on each other for day-to-day affairs." Only one male respondent to the survey mentioned loneliness as a major problem. "Mutual support exists, but it takes time for the exchange," he stated.

Husbands say they work harder to avoid the need for emotional support, but they feel guilty about not providing the emotional protection they believe their wives need. "Loneliness was a tough thing for her," said a middle-income husband. But one partner of a commuter marriage in the hospitality industry insisted, "I know three couples whose marriages wouldn't have survived without commuting. By Sunday evening they're ready to kill each other, but living apart has allowed the marriage to survive and even thrive." Regardless, the implicit comparison between traditional marriage and two-location marriage is always present and is the basis for concerns spouses have regarding their roles in the commuter lifestyle.

The basis for the distinction between "adjusting" couples and "established" couples suggested by Gross (1980) is first of all age. In addition, the length of marriage and the presence of children are important factors. She proposes that adjusting couples are younger, below 38 for husbands and 36 for wives; they have been married for less than 13 years; they have no children. The second group, established couples, are in their late 30s or older; they have been married more than 13 years; they usually have children.

Younger couples struggle with ascendancy conflicts; they wrestle with the dilemma of whose career commitment should predominate. Dick Friedman, 32, describes the struggle between what today's two-career couples are willing to do for love and what they are willing to do for jobs in an article written for *Working Woman*. His hypothetical couple are not so hypothetical. He is outlining his own dilemma. The 34-year-old woman and her 32-year-old husband are living in Philadelphia. She has recently graduated from law school, and he's working for a publishing house. They'd like to stay in Philadelphia, but her best offers are coming from Washington, D.C., and Los Angeles. But in Washington and Los Angeles, jobs for him are nonexistent or not nearly so good as his current job. Starting salaries offered her in these cities are outstanding. So what do they do? If he insists on keeping his job, she'll be relegated to a lesser job in Philadelphia. If she demands that he move, he'll have to scavenge for a lesser job in a strange city. They could both go to New York, where there's no sure thing for either of them but boundless possibilities, or they could decide to commute between two different cities (Friedman 1981:15). The struggle and resulting bitterness could force the marriage to break up. The commuter lifestyle could be a viable alternative, but a great deal of energy is expended in adjusting to it. An article in Ms. called commuting "The Toughest Alternative" (Rhodes and Rhodes 1984).

Meanwhile, the older, established couples with children insist that they have more difficulties with conflict over increased child care and domestic responsibilities for the spouse who stays with the family. "A year ago I left Roger and the baby in our big old house in Iowa," says Mary Crawford (1979). She is describing her experience as a woman raised in a world where married women stayed home. She's now commuting to Iowa from Pennsylvania, her two oldest children are in boarding school in Minnesota, and she's discovered that she is now a "second parent" to her two-year-old son. "It seems to me that he is shamelessly overindulged. I try to straighten him out, Roger and I exchange numerous sharp words, Ben cries and clings to Daddy. I realized I no longer know what it's like dealing with Ben's day-to-day needs. With a shock I see I'm behaving like the stereotype of a male absentee parent." Mary Crawford realizes that she's now less involved and less knowledgeable than her husband when it concerns their two-year-old, and she acknowledges that she feels "guilt, that cradle-to-grave woman's home companion." She feels guilt because she has failed to conform to the cultural expectations of the mother's role; "I know I ought to be there." Roger, meanwhile, breaks down on the phone in tears of weariness and frustration. When these feelings are poured out to a therapist, the response of "Even if you were there, you couldn't make it all better" seems too easy an answer. But Mary finds peace in being able to concentrate on her career, and she has rejected the idea of magical powers given to mothers. She admits that it is not her son's need she feels, but her own (Crawford 1979:76).

Younger Dual-Location Couples: Adjusting

To adopt the "whither thou goest . . . thou goest" attitude is very difficult for the young wife. With greater numbers of women in the work force, their "professional identities" are beginning to be attended to, but for career ascendency to cause psychic stress indicates that women feel the attention to be something extraordinary. As Harriet Gross noted, they are getting an advantage not ordinarily allowed to wives. The commuter wife "is, thus, very 'special' and she knows it." She also feels the accompanying guilt over this treatment that makes her special and "causes him disadvantages relative to other husbands." She is left with the burdensome feeling that somehow she's wronging him (Gross 1980:571). An academic wife "confessed" that she was making great progress on her research and writing while she was commuting, but she felt a terrible compulsion to do laundry, clean the apartment, mop floors, prepare meals, and entertain his business associates when they were together—even when he insisted that she not do any of those things. "The energetic domestic service seemed to be a way that I could make it up to him for allowing me to enjoy my work."

A wife in medical school expresses these same feelings in an interview with Gross. On the one hand she's excited and stimulated to be able to devote herself to her work without having to contend with wifely commitments, but on the other hand, she feels she is hindering her husband's potential. She is not being supportive.

> I was extremely tired but really enjoying myself and I would come home at night and fall into bed. I was very aware of the fact that if he'd been here, you know—relationships take time. There's a good side and a bad side to that—if you don't have time and energy. So I thought, Well, while I'm doing surgery, maybe it's better that Dave's not here. (Gross 1980:572)

Another young wife working on a doctoral degree in business said, "The only place to be when you're writing a dissertation is alone." But she felt conflicting emotions as well. Her husband was alone in California in a brand new position in a university college of business administration. "I know he has some important things he wants to accomplish out there—but the way we're living, I'm not even around to help him get settled. He's very quiet and reluctant to meet new people. I just hope this doesn't hurt his career."

Gross (1980:572) comments that although both take pride in the husband's feminist liberation, the "wife's sense of having something special is, in turn, his sense of having something less." He is giving up the benefits that are seen traditionally as the inalienable right of the male breadwinner, the career-oriented member of the family. None of the male spouses in the survey commented on missing the cooking, cleaning, or other domestic ministrations of the traditional wife even though wives seemed to need to believe they would. What they missed was something much more important. They missed the right to be considered "in first place." To be the one whose career really counted.

Husbands can't acknowledge these feelings openly because they want, truly want, the full development of their wives' intellectual and professional lives, Gross remarks. She notes that in interviews there is frequently a tone of resentment, of diminished self-esteem, and sometimes a sense of embarrassment at appearing to be concerned with wife's career needs. Although a sense of equal partnership exists in the division of domestic labor, when adjusting couples are confronted with the question "Whose career comes first?" underlying the overt response of "equal" or "both" there is frequently the suggestion, "we'll take turns," or "hers now, but mine later." The issue is not whether the wife shall have a career; the majority of male students in university classes and middle-class males in the work force now state that they expect their wives to work. The issue is whose career is more important.

The gaming approach of "we'll take turns" is a hedge that allows retention of male self-image on two levels: first, the recovery of the traditional ascendency of the male breadwinner role; and second, the maintenance of pride in a more participative intimate relationship. Commuting husbands say: "We know this professional couple who have made a decision to alternate, giving each one's career a turn in deciding where to go"; or "At the moment her career comes first, but I hope to have a position with a future—then we will be about equal in importance"; or "My wife's career is more fixed because she owns a business." Women tend to play along with this game, even while maintaining that their careers are important. They say: "My career comes first now because of a better-paying opportunity. We plan to balance these and will make a move for his career if opportunity is better"; or "I'm more overtly ambitious and committed to my career. He tends to express less commitment, but in fact *would not make a move that seriously compromised his work.*" When women executives were polled by a New York executive-search firm, 72 percent said they would give up their positions to relocate for the sake of their husbands' careers, but only 47 percent believed their spouses would do the same for their advancement.

Gross (1980:573) proposed that adjusting couples have two other characteristics that contribute to the career ascendency struggle. First, they have not had the time nor the shared experiences that contribute to a sense of "we-ness." They lack the emotional reservoirs of an enduring long-term marriage. Second, as new, struggling professionals, they have not yet confirmed their professional competence. They still lack the ego strength of their older counterparts. The career power issue becomes more important than the actual fact of living apart. They can't easily say "My career is as important as my marriage" without the underlying feeling of being an "emotional freak." The negative pressures from friends, colleagues, and relatives who question their living apart can be neutralized by seeking friendships with singles and other commuter couples, but the struggles between the partners are more difficult to manage. Especially so since they consciously reject the notion of dominant husband and submissive wife.

Older Dual-Location Couples: Established

Gross sees career clashes of older couples as less violent because they have previously established a solid marital reality. She also suggests that "since they have been married longer, the past usually includes a time when the husband's career did 'come first,' while she stayed at home to raise children and/or work at a 'job' to enable him to succeed." There is now the sense of "correcting an imbalance" in the marital relationship. The wife now feels no guilt in pursuing her own ambitions, since she has "paid her dues." The husband's career is frequently well under way. His competence had been confirmed, and he has less need for ego buttresses. Wives can easily say, "Since my work is in the 'growth' stage, it's important at present—*he has already 'arrived'*" (1980:573).

This same sentiment is expressed by husbands who say, "It's her turn now." These husbands say that the best thing about living together, apart, is "the opportunity it gives my wife to measure up to her potential," "to be the person she's capable of being," "to fulfill herself." Wives say the best thing is "the opportunity to develop independently," "I love the independence." For older couples there is a great sense of satisfaction in seeing the wife blossom, while established husbands react positively to a feeling of payment of obligation for the advantages they previously enjoyed.

Sources of resentment and guilt for these older couples are associated with shifts in parental responsibility, particularly when the children remain with the husband. Gross noted that "Husbands who take pride in their wives' accomplishments still resent the increased child care and household maintenance burdens. Wives, in their turn, miss their children and worry about their lessened input in their children's lives" (1980:574). A commuting wife stated:

I don't know how you balance—I'll be 40 when my last child leaves and that means I have from that point a productive 25 years. I don't know how to balance two or three years of wanting to stay and watch your kids against 30 years of your life. (Gross 1980:574)

For older couples whose career goals involve relocating teenage children, nothing can be quite so tempestuous. "Moving a teenage girl away from her boyfriend can be positively operatic" states Patricia O'Toole (1982:37) in *Savvy* magazine. As recently as 1975 leaving a teenager behind was unheard of; now career women are doing it all the time. If children aren't left with the husband, they are frequently left with friends in the community, and in an increasing number of cases, they are left on their own. One woman noted: "My husband was in Hawaii on a semi-permanent assignment. When I got the offer in Washington at Georgetown, it was too good to turn down. She was determined not to move, and I felt guilty about forcing her. She was almost an adult, 17, and her brother was living in the area. I decided to let her try it on her own. It was a gamble, but she did beautifully. She was happy and I was happy."

Janice and Gordon began commuting when he was given a promotion to a vice presidency with a move to New York. Janice did not want to damage her career at a Midwestern university by giving up her job, and their teenage children didn't want to leave their home and friends in the Midwest. At times before making the decision to commute, they tentatively but seriously talked about whether their marriage should continue. Eventually they decided that their marriage could continue on a new and different basis and that they could live in different places. When they examined their life, they became aware that they had been spending only an hour, or less, per day in actual sharing of activities. Sometimes they didn't see each other at all; during the week Janice often had late classes, and Gordon would get up early for work and occasionally stay late for business meetings. Living apart, now they spend two or three weekends a month together, and the children sometimes go to New York with Janice. After analyzing the quantity and quality of their time together, they have ceased to feel guilty about their new family relationship. They have discovered that they are working harder than ever at improving the quality of the hours they do have.

The Benders are good examples of established commuters, although they are pioneers in the still chancy business of commuter marriage. Bill is 48, and Sally is 40. Each morning Bill fixes breakfast for Margaret, 15, and Sarah, 7, and then he drives Sarah to public school, where he receives a cordial good morning from mothers who drop off their children at the same time. Sometimes people say to Bill, "My hat's off to you," thereby acknowledging his role in child care as unusual, if not downright deviant or some sort of martyrdom. Bender then returns home, makes the beds, does the dishes, and tries to settle down to the life of a writer in the midst of household distractions. "That's the part that isn't easy," he says. Bill feels guilty if he gets lazy and opens a can of Spaghetti-Os for Sarah, and Sally feels guilty if she sneaks a cigarette in her tiny 14-foot-square Washington efficiency where the landlord doesn't allow her to smoke. Otherwise the couple have few qualms about their two-city lifestyle

and role reversals. Sally Bender states, "If people don't understand, I don't entertain their conversation." Bill Bender agrees.
"It's a fantastic opportunity for Sally and I wouldn't want her to
miss it. We're doing fine" (O'Brien 1979:1c).

And indeed, established commuters tend to do somewhat better than their adjusting counterparts. The Gross study
of 28 dual-location marriages concluded that the trade-offs the
two types make are not equally discomfiting. Three things seem
to make coping easier for the older couples: (1) the solidity of
their relationship, (2) the faith that they can endure the demands of living apart, and (3) the recognition that they are
compensating for the wife's past efforts on the husband's behalf. Naomi Gerstel and Harriet Gross have a full discussion of
adjusting and established commuters in their book, *Commuter
Marriage*: A *Study of Work and Family* (1984).

Meanwhile, George Hughston and Terri Eisler (1984) believe there are three types of commuter couples. Rather than
basing their categories on age, length of marriage, and the presence of children as do Gerstel and Gross, they look at the motivation underlying the choice to commute.

Hughston and Eisler believe that one type of commuter
marriage is based on the need for a joint income to maintain a
lifestyle and the difficulty of finding two jobs in one location.
Long-distance marriage for this group is "financially induced."
The couple lives together, apart, because they have to. A second
type, the "complementary career," is made up of couples so
professionally oriented they are unable to give up one career in
order to satisfy the other. The third group is what Hughston and
Eisler call the "pseudo-divorce." Commuter marriage is chosen
by these couples because they are headed for a split up—
whether they know it or not. They stay married for the children
or because it is easier than going through the trauma and financial problems of divorce. While couples in the first two groups
may have strong relationships, family and friends, co-workers,
and employers frequently view all long-distance marriage as
pseudo-divorce, thereby weakening the support system two-city
couples need. The pseudo-divorce category is generalized to all
commuters and prevents societal changes that would genuinely

make two engrossing jobs, two residences, and a rewarding relationship less bizarre.

"Syndromes" Affecting Commuter Couples

Because commuter couples are definitely breaking the established rules of the culture concerning what a family should be, they are under enormous pressure to "make it work." Their exotic lifestyle has to be justified by success; so they fall prey to, or at the very least are in danger of succumbing to, a number of symptoms that characterize specific conditions. A few of them are described below.

The Supermom, Superdad, Supersuccess Syndrome

This condition is also known as "role overload." A role overload victim will talk like this: "I think both Doug and I put a lot of energy into being with the kids so they get enough attention. I find that sometimes at night, when I'm tired, I have to resist the temptation to 'tune out,' especially at that crucial time when the kids need to talk about some earth-shattering event in the seventh grade."

Women tend to feel responsible for everything. On the one hand, two-career marriages accept the need for setting priorities, but on the other they are under pressure to "get everything done." If not, they feel guilty about their competence. They are always trying to please someone else and rarely sit back and ask themselves, "What do I want?" Supermoms assume both practical and emotional responsibility. For example, if it is the husband's job to shop for the groceries, that is his *practical* responsibility. But if his wife feels she has to prod him to do it, or if she worries about whether he does the job perfectly, she's taking on the *emotional* responsibility. Supermom or superdad symptoms are a direct result of traditional role expectations hidden in the marriage contract.

Most articles and books written to "help" working moms do little more than deepen the guilt by giving trivial advice on "strategies for coping." One article designed to make working and commuting moms repent their sins noted that "because a working mother has less time for her children, it is important for her to stay as involved as possible with their activities at school" (Gaylin 1983:19). This is the accepted idea that mothers have sole responsibility for children. This approach looks merely at the superficial aspect of "less time," but it is quite reasonable to consider as well the qualitative aspects of time spent with children. Supermoms, however, never do.

The focus of the "super" syndrome has traditionally been on mom, but as we hear more about the role of the father in parenting, dads are being let into the ranks. They can become "superdads." The reapportionment of tasks helps to make a superdad. One woman interviewed stated that "behind every successful woman there is a man." She was not referring so much to her husband's tackling the practical tasks such as shopping, laundry, cooking, and child minding. She was referring to his encouraging her by giving advice on how to cope with problems at work. He was providing consultation and had taken on the career guidance function. In a traditional one-career, one-household marriage the wife supplies the domestic "backup." Now the husband must, or feels he must, assume this emotional responsibility. Then, of course, for the commuter dad, there is the guilt-producing absence from children if they are not living with him. If they are, he must try very much harder than his wife might to be assured that he is doing even an average job of "mothering" his children.

Whether a couple acquires the "supersuccess" syndrome depends upon the degree to which they aspire to both a high standard of domestic living and a high standard of career achievement. When a couple wants a pleasant home, a garden, gourmet cooking, and *House Beautiful* decor, the problem of managing becomes difficult. If their career objectives are "top of the ladder" as well, the supersuccess syndrome is hard to avoid. A commuting wife relates her supersuccess symptoms in this way: "We were determined to go to the top because we enjoyed our jobs, maybe more than younger couples since both of us were on our second careers. I was a homemaker-mother dropout with a challenging new position in university teaching, and Dave was beginning a new career in tourism management after teaching for thirty years. When Dave was sent to Palm Springs, I stayed at the university, and I'd drive 650 miles every weekend. Well, sometimes Dave would drive, but my schedule was more flexible, so it was easier for me to be away. Anyway, we rented a nice sun-belt type garden apartment and kept our house here. But it suddenly seemed to me that neither place ever looked right. The garden here became shabby, and I was almost a day late getting on the road to see Dave one weekend while I tried to save the vegetable crop, which hadn't been taken in early enough to save it from the first hard frost. Then I'd get to Palm Springs and the kitchen floor seemed dingy and the bathroom didn't shine. How could I have the Rogers over to dinner with the place like that? I felt like one of those women in the commercials who never seem to get it right. I was being surrounded by rings-around-the-collar. And then, when I'd get back to the university on Monday afternoon, so much seemed to have happened while I was gone that I felt out of touch. I wasn't, but it seemed like it. At first, I tried to get Dave to keep the Palm Springs place up to my standards, but it didn't work. He thought it was *okay*. Finally, I began to look at it in a different way. If I had been going off for a great romantic weekend with a lover, or if I were going to be visiting a good friend, would I complain or even notice the kitchen floor? Of course not! So what difference did it make? We were happy, and we had much better ways to spend our time than trying to reach the unrealistic ideal depicted in *Sunset Magazine* and promoted by Madison Avenue."

The importance of having children and the willingness to delegate child care is also a contributing factor in overload. The supermom, superdad, and supersuccess overload syndromes lead eventually to an even more difficult situation, fatigue fallout.

The Fatigue Fallout Syndrome

"Parenthood and Career Overtax Some Women Despite Best Intentions" read the headline of a 1983 *Wall Street Journal* page one article. In the seventies the problem seemed to be finding qualified women managers. Now the problem is retaining women managers. "I felt split loyalty," says Barbara Keck, an M.B.A. from Harvard. Barbara got up at 6:30 A.M., rode the train for an hour from New York to Stamford, spent her lunch hour feeding the baby, who stayed with a sitter in Stamford, and got home at 8 P.M. Exhausted, she asked her employer for part-time hours, and when the company refused, she quit (Toman 1983:1).

For all commuter couples physical exhaustion is an important issue. They emphasize the absolute need for good health as a prerequisite for the lifestyle. And children are supposed to be healthy too. There simply isn't room in the system for illness. One mother said, "I knew it was going to be a difficult situation for a while. I told the kids, 'This year we simply don't have *time* to be sick,' and you know, they never were. We went the whole year without illness, not even a runny nose, except for Annie and she waited until the Easter holiday." Dual-career commuter living may decrease the medical bills, since there is not time to be sick and even less time to sit in doctors' offices. The system has very little slack, and little energy is left for extra activities. The success that dual-career, dual-location couples have in maintaining good health may well be attibutable to their mental outlook more than to any physical factors. Viruses don't have time to catch up with them; they're moving too fast.

The emphasis on health is evident from the large number of commuters who engage in sports. Many are competitive tennis players, swimmers, or joggers. One 55-year-old displays fifteen trophies in her office. She confided that she enjoys the supportive spirit of fellow runners in the large ten-kilometer road races, but she admitted she also likes to leave at least some of the 20- and 30-year-olds behind. "We swim, sail, ride bikes, and run a lot," says a New York–San Francisco commuter. "Eventually, my adrenaline is going to wear out."

The commuter lifestyle taxes the stamina of even the most addicted workaholics. Many work 14- to 18-hour days during the week living in hotel rooms, travel trailers, or small apartments. Frequently the week is spent eating TV dinners or deli sandwiches. On Friday morning, Friday afternoon for the less flexible schedules, there is the dash to the airport or the race to the car and from there to their partners and "home." On Monday morning, it's back again to the long hours during the day and the long-distance phone at night. Inevitably, the routine exacts physical and psychological cost. One couple describes their relationship as "almost entirely an energy thing." "You do run out of steam. We're amazed sometimes that we have survived until the holidays." Not everyone makes it. They are simply too tired. But only a few considered that the drain on physical energy incurred by frequent traveling is a major issue. The commitment to work, especially for established couples, is so well fixed that dropping out seems unthinkable.

The Intermittent Husband or Wife Syndrome

Every culture distinguishes different subphases or role cycles. For instance, we name certain phases that the family passes through: engagement, honeymoon, marriage, parenthood, widowhood. When a young man marries, he enters the role of husband and he has a cycle of experiences in that role. When he takes on the additional role of father, he has another cycle of experiences. When the children leave home, he must disengage from the father role. Psychologists and sociologists (see Rossi 1968:29) think of the role cycle as having four phases: the "anticipatory" phase, which is a preparation for the role; the "honeymoon" phase, which is the early establishment and stabilization of the ways of managing the role; the "plateau" or steady-state phase, during which the role is fully developed; and the "disengagement" phase, in which the role is given up either voluntarily or under the force of circumstances (Fogarty, Rapoport, and Rapoport 1971:364).

The parental role is one into which women are pushed by cultural expectations while men are thrust into the role of breadwinner. Among commuting families young couples are particularly susceptible to role cycle and role transition difficulties because they are still in the "honeymoon" phase in both career and family. A particularly bad situation is one in which a working wife is catapulted into becoming a parent accidentally or stampeded into motherhood by cultural pressures before her career is established and before the family can afford domestic help. Compromises become necessary for males as well. One husband interviewed who had just begun to succeed in his career stated, "I certainly felt that being married to someone who has her own successful real estate business would be great—until my company asked me to relocate. Suddenly my ability to take risks and be brave and bold about my immediate career was curbed. I had married, had a child, and my wife was anxious to maintain her career. I thought I'd bitten off more than I could chew."

The major dilemma for older commuters is role transition. For example, Sally had learned to cope with her husband's regular two-week absences from home. She runs the household; she is successful in her clerical position; she has adjusted to loneliness; she manages to take care of three small children, playing the father's role as well as the mother's. She is no longer in the honeymoon stage of the role cycle but has achieved the plateau stage in which her role is fully developed. But much to her distress, she now finds she is having trouble coping with the regular periods when her husband is back in town. "It doesn't seem fair for him just to walk back in and take over his old role again," she confides. "I can't keep making this transition from completely dependent on him to running the whole show." Sally feels guilt, depression, and anxiety because she is not happy over her husband's return. Commuter couples aren't the only ones who face the "intermittent husband and wife syndrome." Military, diplomatic, truck driver, and oil rig wives, to name only a few, have all reported that they feel more relaxed when their husbands are away once they have become accustomed to getting along on their own. Adjusting to widowhood or divorce has received a great deal of attention from psychiatrists, but adjusting to a returning husband or more recently a returning wife is just now beginning to be investigated.

A *New York Times* article noted: "Dr. Richard A. Isay, studying the wives of submarine crewmen at the United States Naval Base in Groton, Conn., found a pattern of moodiness and upset in the weeks just before the husband's return from his time at sea. . . . He and other doctors studying the problem have found that such symptoms as uncontrolled weeping and headaches sometimes coincide with the husband's return. And in the longer term, they relate the problem to alcoholism and sexual promiscuity as well." Psychiatrists propose that it is the way of life that produces these symptoms. "Much that is classified as neurotic actually has to do with the inadequacy of the social network" (Borders 1980).

The lack of social support may be important, of course (see chapter 4), but something more basic is involved, and that is the primacy of the roles themselves. It is a matter of power. Since the husband-father role carries more clout, the husband comes home and reasserts his authority over the children. He seeks to establish his wife's role in the home as secondary once again. It's not entirely unreasonable to suppose that a wife who is about to lose control, to abdicate authority, to move from a dominant role to a subservient one might indeed be moody and even prone to uncontrollable tears. The husband may use his sexual relationship with his wife in a political way as well. But reasserting authority doesn't always work; so he leaves after an unpleasant time at home worrying about his marriage while she worries about her reaction to him.

With two-location, two-career couples, the situation can be reversed. When the children remain with the father and the mother returns home on weekends, she is apt to plunge into her "Mommy" role and resent being a "second parent" (Crawford 1979). But overall, two-career families deal with role cycling and role transition somewhat more successfully than single-career traditional male breadwinner families where the husband's career determines absence. Intermittent husbands often insist that wives not work because "when I'm in town I want her to devote all of her time to me"; then wives say, "but what do I do with all my time while he's gone?" (Borders 1980). The answer for these women is role overload; they play both "supermom" and "superdad." Two-career commuters simply don't have time for this. Domestic roles may not loom as quite so large when there are demanding career roles for both husband and wife. Then too, since both work, the division of domestic labor may be less rigid and the traditional role boundaries less well defined.

The Identity Syndrome

The symptoms here arise from a very deep level and are internally generated conficts concerning whether one is a "good" man, a "good" woman, or a "good" person. Definitions of good people come from cultural ideas of work and family as intrinsically masculine and feminine. The essence of masculinity is still centered on work and competing successfully in the head-of-household role. The essence of femininity is still centered on the domestic scene even as we approach the 60 percent rate for female participation in the work force. There are a few acceptable occupations where women can still be "real" women—nursing, teaching in the lower grades or possibly even high school, social work, and lower-level clerical positions. Conversely, when men enter these occupations the encounter internal identity problems. One young man stated that his nursing career ended before it began because of the language of the catalogs and textbooks in nursing school. Everything was "she." For example, "During *her* studies, *she* assumes responsibilities in keeping with *her* stage of learning." The English language itself prevents us from changing our thought patterns even when we wish to change. Women encounter identity problems when they become "businessmen," and men encounter problems when they become "housewives."

Commuter couples look at the husband and wife roles from the viewpoint of traditional single-career marriage and the unwritten marriage contract. This is especially true for younger, adjusting couples. Lacking a new model, the exotic two-city family compares itself with "real" marriage (people who live together) to see if the partners are "real" men and women. But since they are being very modern and enlightened about these things, what actually happens is that they can go to a certain distance toward establishing the new individual identities they have designed for themselves outside the sociocultural pressures, but discomfort arises under certain circumstances. They can experiment only so far, and then the traditional sex role definitions take over. There is a limit beyond which experimentation seems unable to go without damaging the male or female sense of self-esteem. These limits have been called "tension lines" (Fogarty, Rapoport, and Rapoport 1971:357).

Manifestations of tension lines are sometimes very subtle. Margaret, 54, and her husband Troy, 57, were both teaching in middle-sized universities, he in the Southeast and she in the

Southwest. In order to have more time together, they frequently contributed papers to the same conferences, where they could meet as an extra special bonus outside the usual vacation time. Troy welcomed and encouraged his wife's participation in these activities that furthered her career. He wanted above all for her to achieve her career ambitions. Margaret, however, confesses that she could never feel comfortable lecturing at a conference or in a classroom when her husband was present. "I'm very authoritarian in the classroom or when I talk about my research. I sometimes put on quite a show. I'm not really sure which is the real me. The one who stands in front of an audience, the one wearing jeans when we're together hunting or cooking, or the one in the black lace nightie." Where occupational goals call for aggressive behavior inconsistent with conceptions of the wifely role, women become uncomfortable and seem to retreat into the kitchen where they can be sure to be "good" wives. Margaret may also be fearful of criticism from her higher-ranking husband. She may have been wary of the possible backlash of feelings stemming from the sacrifices she felt Troy was making in order to support her in her professional life.

Another way women deal with this tension line when they feel they give too much emphasis to their career ambitions is to play down the ambitions. They present their career as a string of random occurrences rather than a series of steps taken toward a career goal. Things simply happen *to* them. They are the passive recipients rather than the active agents in professional identity. The fact is, few wives will admit to career goals. For example, one woman stated, "I wanted the job so much I felt sick to my stomach. But when it came right down to it I was overwhelmed. It meant leaving my family. All these years I've thought of myself as an independent, aggressive woman, but when it came down to the last minute, I couldn't make the break."

The sexual identity tension line for men can be recognized in often unnoticed undercutting behavior by the husband toward the wife. The "it's her turn now" behavior of established commuter couples has a touch of this. That is, the husband feels totally secure in his masculine identity; so now he will "allow" her to try. Or, husbands will make something of a joke of their wives' business practices. The husband of a real estate woman remarked, "She's not making that much." Dual-career couples almost universally made some attempt to divide the domestic chores between them. But the most frequent complaint over a small task comes with "not wiping down the kitchen counters." "He tries to help me in the kitchen. When I cook, he does the cleanup, but he *never* wiped off the kitchen counters! I finally couldn't take it, so I mentioned it. He was all apology. He'd never thought about it . . . didn't notice. So he promised to do better. Now he mops up the counters leaving a lake of water that could float the Loch Ness monster." It's clear that shining up kitchen counters is stepping over the bounds into something that "good" males don't do. It is hard to avoid the notion that good women stay home and good men go to work. It is much harder yet to avoid the idea that "good marriages" are those in which people live together.

Preserving the concept of one's marriage as "good" is achieved almost universally by commuters through insisting on the notion that "it is only a temporary situation." "Someday we'll get together." "We're only going to do this until Ralph finds a job here." The ideal is to someday find positions in the same location. Until then, everything is "on ice" with a "someday my prince will come" attitude. Again it is traditional marriage that is the model, and viewing traditional marriage as the ideal way prevents couples from working out a satisfactory and rewarding nontraditional marriage. Rita and Martin are one of these couples. Martin is a psychology professor in Virginia and Rita has a postdoctoral fellowship in Maine. They plan to continue the long-distance relationship only until Rita finishes in Maine, and then they hope to locate two jobs in the same community. Martin says, "I wouldn't go on with it forever. Marriage is a chance to spend time with a single individual. It doesn't fit my definition of marriage."

But maybe the definition is an outdated one. With more women in the permanent work force, who is going to make the career sacrifice? Definitions can change, and they are changing for some couples. Beyond cultural definitions of what is a good man, a good woman, a good marriage, there is a notion of a personal identity. That identity can be lost if a career is sacrificed. For example, Beatrice thought of her husband as the primary breadwinner, and when Teasdale Coal Co. wanted him, she gave up her position in journalism to follow. "I seemed to have lost something more than the work that I loved. My identity. I became a Company wife, and even though I had a part-time replacement job, it was only symbolic."

The Hidden Paycheck Syndrome

Tension lines are encountered for some families in the matter of income. There is a crucial point that develops if the wife's income is greater than the husband's. The problem, as Caroline Bird (1979) notes, begins with her paycheck. Since she isn't supposed to have one, tradition doesn't say what to do with it. There can be a strain on the relationship if a woman is promoted faster than her husband. The usual way of avoiding this is not to talk about it. Everyone becomes silent: husbands, wives, insurance companies, family finance advisers, savings banks. Managing money can be a form of communication in itself. Look at what the government does. Courts assume that anything bought with money was bought with *his* money. This makes a joint ownership of property a trap unless couples take very complicated precautions. The law minimizes the wife's earnings by making the husband head-of-household even if she earns more or even when both marriage partners tell the census taker or the Internal Revenue Service that they regard her as head-of-household. Separate credit reports are still clumsy to come by even with recent changes in reporting and changes in the law.

The Motivational Syndrome

"Why am I doing this anyway?" For the commuter couples it is pretty clear that financial security is not a major factor except for middle-income couples who have been forced to live apart because of economic crisis. But many women, like many men, have come to see their level of earnings as some kind of measure of personal worth in the world. Some women who are highly career motivated seem to have experienced early economic deprivation, and they are very much aware that this is a factor driving them toward a goal of economic security. Other women who at one time relied upon the security of a husband's career but who later found themselves widowed or divorced, "displaced homemakers," are reluctant to put themselves in such a vulnerable position again when they remarry. Connie was one of these. She was 52 when she met Robert. She'd been divorced for 12 years and had established herself in a prestigious management position. The problem was, Connie and Robert lived on separate sides of the country. "I wasn't about to put myself into a situation where I was ever again dependent upon a man. I loved Robbie and I guess I trusted him, but once was enough. No more giving up a secure, interesting job for what might not be such a secure relationship. We both kept our jobs, and we commute on holidays. It's lovely." Two-city couples commute less for financial gain than for personal career interests.

Commuter wives are no more masculine and commuter husbands are no more feminine than traditional ones. The couples do not diverge behaviorally from traditional patterns. They may be somewhat more independent, but the women are no more dominant and tough-minded nor are the men more high-strung and erratic in performance than in traditional couples. Agnes Farris (1978) found that what does seem to be different is enjoyment of a lifestyle characterized by compartmentalization of work and home life. In her research with commuting couples, she noted that "During the days away from home the commuter is totally involved in work, long hours, busy schedules, full concentration on work without interference from family demands. During the weekend, time and attention are devoted to family oriented activities, spending time with husband or wife and children, helping out in household chores." For some, just the family shopping becomes an occasion. For others, it's enjoying nature together. Commuters seem to enjoy the total segregation of work from home life. They like to live in two worlds.

The major motivation of commuter couples seems to be the meaning of work for them as individuals. It is a part of their overall mental health program. Amy, 33, had taken a position that was part-time when she left her job in order to be with Paul in Los Alamos. She said, "I felt I'd lost my own separate sphere." So she decided she had to get back into her work even if it was at a long distance. Paul encouraged her to go for an interview "When I did, I found myself in love again with working on a newspaper." Work for commuter couples is generally a form of self-expression. It is essential for their self-conception. "People ask me why I'm smiling, and I can't tell them *what* the smile is all about. It's just great to have a job that brings me so much to smile about," Amy admitted.

One couple who had solved the job problem by sharing one professorship at a rural college found that being each other's closest colleague wasn't working. "We needed to develop individual approaches to our work. . . . We needed to pursue private career interests. Paradoxically, we'd come to share too much. A little distance was in order. My pleasure now comes from my work, my solitude, and my friends," says the wife.

With all the success that may come to a spouse in a commuter marriage from working the 10, 12, 14-hour day, there seems to be one major drawback that at least most of them feel is very real. It is the loneliness and the lack of a supportive spouse handily beside them to share the daily triumphs and sorrows. "I miss sharing the emotional things as well as the obvious physical things. You forfeit a certain amount of closeness. The vital day-to-day communication is gone," says a commuting attorney. "We coped with commuting because we had to, but there was always the deep sensation that we were missing something," says a commuting management consultant.

The "something missing" is a symptom of a minor disorder known as the "alone at the top syndrome." Men seem more susceptible to the syndrome than women because in a commuter marriage the man gives up the traditional wifely support system that exists in even the most egalitarian situation where wives still nurture the relationship. Men resent it, because it's not what they bargained for. The trouble is, both partners sacrifice. What they both need is a "wife." One wife says, "The problem that was ever present and didn't seem to lessen with time was loneliness, although I had friends who invited me to dinner, accompanied me to movies, and were properly supportive when my morale needed boosting." Serious upward-striving people need to be geographically mobile, but sometimes when friends and business associates find out that the spouse is not around, they handle the situation awkwardly. Mark, in San Francisco, found that when his wife Dixie moved to Los Angeles with an airline organization he suddenly became persona non grata to couples they had been close to. Dixie, meanwhile, had to limit socializing to business necessities because the would-be swains were becoming insistent.

Commuting can also limit business growth and cause lost opportunities. Roger said, "I can't lead a project team for the simple reason that I'm not in my office every day. Some people don't even want me on their teams for that reason." Another feels that his business growth is limited since he has to rush off to drive 90 miles each weekend and can't do the last-minute work or make the extra contacts that might help his public relations business. The problem that seems most serious for all commuters is the one of building a social arrangement that creates for the individual the sort of order in which life can make sense. Berger and Keller in their article "Marriage and the Construction of Reality" (1967:3) note that the reality-bestowing force of social relationships depends on the degree of their nearness, that is, on the degree to which social relationships occur in face-to-face contexts and also the degree to which they are credited with primary significance by the individuals.

Chapter Three

"And Forsaking All Other, Cleave Thee Only Unto . . ."

Sex and the Married Single

"**O**ur arrangement does include sexual freedom," he said. Michael, 29, and Cindy, 26, were both teaching school in Boston three years ago when they decided to move to Portland. But only Michael was able to move there. They see each other three times a year. Michael believes that their new way of life has totally changed his views about marriage. Cindy agrees. "Our decision was mutual," she admitted. "We talked it over and discovered that we would both enjoy being free to become involved sexually with someone else if we needed that kind of physical and emotional support while we were apart. I truly couldn't see myself living like a nun just because Michael wasn't around. I'm a very social kind of person. We both enjoy singles bars. We used to go when we were together." Michael says, "Our marriage is good and strong and I don't doubt for one minute that everything will work out. If you believe it . . . it'll be."

Married singles are assumed not to exist. But they have been around for a long time in *male-determined* two-location families. Salesmen, soldiers, male immigrants, and business executives have historically spent much time in hotel rooms, barracks, and boarding houses while still accepting the notion that they began their most recent commuting, Max took the night shift. He says he enjoyed working nights because there was less tendency to go for drinks with the other workers. He'd get up from his day sleeping at just the prime bar time, and he states, "I didn't want to go to work intoxicated, so I worked nights and stayed away from the whole thing and saved myself a lot of money and trouble." Irene feels strongly about their money going to taverns and says she wouldn't tolerate a relationship like that. They both think that jealousy isn't good, that you must have a trusting relationship and be very loyal, but Irene insists, "Our commuter marriage wouldn't have worked if Max had been working the day shift and I suspected that he was going to the bars."

Another commuter couple in their late 30s, Al and Marie, said they believed in loyalty and in talking things over. They said that their decision on extramarital relations when they were separated was a firm no. But Al admits sheepishly that "Her answer was '*no*', while I said 'whatever'." Things aren't always as they seem even after discussion. Marie hadn't been aware that Al was hedging. They had been apart before while he was on temporary assignment, and in discussing fidelity he admitted, "Well, there were, uh, . . . we had one or two."

"Oh, have *we*?" said Marie.

"In the *far, far* distant past," Al added quickly.

When asked about extramarital relations, most couples respond, "Why jeopardize a beautiful marriage?" "It's not a matter of permitting; it's a matter of loyalty, health, and wasted time on short-term flings." The consensus seems to be that extramarital affairs aren't worth it. Besides, commuter couples are highly time conscious. With almost every moment essential to the efficient achievement of career and family goals, there may simply not be enough physical and emotional energy left to think about it, let alone do anything about it. One woman whose commuter marriage permits outside relationships confided that with her spouse gone (they are able to commute only every other month) she misses sex because "I rarely run into attractive men." She admits she hasn't the time for looking, but believes they must be around somewhere.

Nevertheless, there is still a double standard that says it may be fine for a man to live apart from his family (the traveling salesman mental set), but a woman must never do so. Peggy van Hulsteyn reported in *Mademoiselle* that when she was looking for an advertising job she came across a creative director who reacted with horror to the news that she was commuting. When she nonchalantly explained that situation to him, he became almost enraged and exclaimed, "Boy I wouldn't allow my wife to do anything like that! Does your husband know you are here?" (Van Hulsteyn 1978:86). Although most couples say that their new way of life has changed their views on marriage, most freely admit, "Our arrangement does not include sexual freedom."

Researchers insist that commuters do not have any more affairs than stay-at-home couples. So much concentration is poured into work and marriage that there is little energy left over for it. Obviously, women who were once upon a time limited to the milkman or the golf instructor now have the same opportunities for misbehavior as the men have had all along, but fatigue can put restrictions on extramarital affairs.

Commuter couples are loyal, and there is generally a high degree of fidelity despite frequent absence from one another that allows plenty of opportunity for extramarital relations. So does that mean commuters are also routine, that they are traditional in their sexual relationships? Not so. Commuter couples have some interesting things to say about their feast-or-famine sex lives. But the truth is that most tend to rule out sexual jealousy because such doubts consume too much energy in an eventful two-location marriage.

Biographical statements from two-city couples seem to take two major positions on how commuting affects their sex lives. Most feel that separation improves the sexual relationship, but some criticize the romantic idea of long-distance marriage and stress the loneliness, exhaustion, and expense. Let's first look at some of the statements that speak of the "return of romance," and then at some of the problems in meeting intimacy needs. Finally, we may see how commuter marriage, by defying conventional societal attitudes and pressures, can allow the expression of full sexuality.

Cleveland: When It Sizzles

Long-distance love means: "romantic Dom Pérignon homecomings, dreamy, sexy nights following dinner tête-à-tête, while in between these lush, cherished liaisons you have the emotional support of a husband plus your independence, your privacy, your identity as an individual and not as an appendage to somebody else" (Van Hulsteyn 1978:86).

Somewhat lyric? Maybe. Let's try this one: "There's a lot more sacrifice involved than you'd imagine. It's not a relationship. It's a *weekend romance*. It's not a marriage." Reading this, you begin to wonder exactly what is a marriage anyway, and what is a romance, and why must the two be mutually exclusive. Marriage begins to sound utilitarian. Romance begins to sound very sinful, but also very special. Maybe romance and marriage are not two separate worlds for commuter couples.

An ex-commuter whose husband had at last succeeded in relocating said that it was delightful to be together all the time, but "sometimes when the air smells just right on an early Friday morning, and the sun is shining brightly, I long to hit the road across the high Arizona desert and feel the excitement and suspense of going off to see my love and have the intense weekend days we had back then." Commuters feel compelled to plan their precious weekends with extra care. Time becomes quality time.

A *Wall Street Journal* article described the reaction of Securities and Exchange Commissioner Barbara Thomas and her husband, a New York attorney. "The first hour on Friday evening is shared going through the week's mail. There's a lot of business we want to get out of the way first, including coordinating our schedules where necessary. From then on, we concentrate on our relationship." Mrs. Thomas calls their weekends together "sacred" but concedes that she cannot relax fully because she feels extra responsibility to make the times together special (Langley 1981:1).

Couples seem to agree that "You just cannot pick up where you left off." There is a reentry period or reacquaintance period, and one way of coping is to turn the reunion into a new courtship. And it's exciting. Sarah Conn, a clinical psychologist who runs workshops for two-career couples in Newton, Massachusetts, says that "This person who shows up on Friday night is not the old familiar person whose dirty socks have been hanging around for a week. There's a newness comparable to going out on a first date." Marvin Whaley, who works in ad sales for a radio station in Atlanta and is half of a St. Louis–Atlanta marriage, told *Time*: "When you're together, it's all prime-time." With increasing airline costs and high telephone bills, the Whaleys have tried to cut down on expenses. Nevertheless, Marvin sent Robin a singing telegram that cost $45 instead of one week's phone calls (Leo 1982:84). It is this kind of gallantry that makes commuter marriages, commuter romances.

Fatigue can limit the sex lives of commuter couples. Couples who say they fantasize all week, or all month, about exotic sexual bouts are surprised to find they prefer sitting by the fire, or holding hands in front of the TV. They climb wearily into bed only to cuddle together and sleep spoon fashion. But, "You make up for it on vacations."

"Whenever I went home, it was like a two-day honeymoon into which we tried to pack all the fun and excitement we could." In the opinion of Marvin B. Sussman, head of the Department of Medical Social Sciences at the Bowman Gray School of Medicine, Winston-Salem, N.C., commuting couples can block out a lot of the garbage that goes into a relationship and concentrate on renewing involvement with each other (U.S. *News and World Report* 1977:110).

Commuters propose that while the frequency of sex obviously decreases, the periods of absence lead to more excitement. "Being together is exciting and romantic." "Obviously, there is more appreciation for each other because we get so little." "It has made it [sex] extremely exciting—especially after a three-week separation."

One commuter stated that the long-distance relationship enhanced sexual pleasure at times and detracted from it at other times, since more importance was sometimes placed upon performance because of lack of time together; but this lack of time also creates the situation in which "When you're there, you're really there!" Other couples suggest that pressure for sexual "performance" is lessened in a commuter relationship. Since there is not a day-to-day intimacy, there is no expectation for daily, every-other-day, or any other sort of scheduled sexual activity. Sexual performance for these couples becomes more spontaneous and more natural during their "honeymoon" times together.

Romance isn't adult toys, nighties, spouse swapping, or even warm nights on a Caribbean island sipping dark rum drinks served in coconut shells topped with colorful Japanese paper parasols. It is an equal partnership, having the courage to care, thinking about and especially planning for valuable time together. This may be difficult, if not impossible, in a day-to-day situation, where who will bring in the firewood, clean the garage, or discipline the children often takes precedence.

Of course, commuting is much easier and possibly much more romantic as well if you both happen to be successful corporation executives. Dick and Jane are an example. They live 3,000 miles apart. She's in New York and he's in California. They have a flourishing marriage and are both "moving up the ladder of promotion" in their firms. They both have a deep respect for one another's individuality. They do not seek to make one another over into the other's image, but they have a single aim to achieve a partnership of great closeness and mutual care. Jane and Dick say that "Respect for one another will nurture greater understanding of love, but only if you both so desire." Their commuting plans are elaborate and call for meeting at least once a month while they engage in one of their favorite avocations—travel. The couple has a list of exotic trysting places on every continent where they indulge in their other leisure activities, such as scuba diving and flying. Be it the Casbah, Sahara, or Baja California, they maximize their limited time together with fun (Dexter 1977:6).

It's not essential, however, to travel around the world to find romantic situations. Roz and Brian do it with back packs, a tent, and some imagination. Roz commutes to Utah, where Brian teaches. On weekends they hike into isolated stretches of beach on the shores of Lake Powell, where they cook the fish they catch, skinny-dip, and watch the sunrise over Monument

Valley. They play fantasy games with each other: Cave Dweller, Anastasi Indian, and "Me Tarzan, You Jane." But Brian says they are sometimes just quietly together, thinking and reading.

The excitement value of sexual practices is lessened for traditional one-city couples because sexual excitement is often related to obstacles. Boredom can result when all barriers are eliminated. As obstacles increase for two-city couples, so does sexual pleasure.

Topeka: When It Drizzles

The criticism of the romantic vision of long-distance marriage stresses the loneliness, fatigue, and financial disadvantages of commuting. It refutes the idea of a marriage existing at all and proposes that long-distance marriage lacks the intimacy of a long-term relationship and is merely a good way to spend the weekend. Indeed, there is a great deal of sacrifice involved, but despite the drawbacks, separation may be necessary to career fulfillment and self-actualization. The *New York Times* recounted the story of Jan Hodgson and her husband James Bergfalk, who made the difficult decision to live apart for career fulfillment. Jan stated "I'm the kind of person—my husband is too—who needs to be challenged, stimulated, and interested in my daily work. Even though I was happy being with him, I was unhappy in my work, and that worried him." So Jan lives in Kansas City and James lives 150 miles northwest in Jefferson City, and despite the loneliness and fatigue of commuting they have few regrets (Rule 1977:60).

This is not the case with some single-residence, two-career couples, such as the situation Elisabeth Perry (1983:64) describes. She talks about the "unhappy lot" of the two-career academic marriage that suffers not only from the general lack of academic jobs but also from the terrible need to find *two* academic jobs in the same community. Dr. Perry says you can scratch the surface of any academic community and find plenty of cases of unemployed or underemployed academic spouses (mostly females). The struggle for a position can last for ten or fifteen or more years and the job never materialize. She speaks of "hurtful experience," "insensitive colleagues," and of an attitude of "yet we endure . . . being careful not to wallow in self-pity." To cope with the lack of meaningful work, Dr. Perry suggests "staying loose" and "being aggressive (but not too!)." But the patience, flexibility, and cautious self-promotion advocated may not be enough to allow a two-career marriage to survive. It is certainly not a situation in which there is the equal partnership that allows romantic sexuality to thrive. When one partner has opted for career sacrifice, the couple may not be able to "live happily ever after" with that choice. Elisabeth Perry wasn't, and she found an alternative; she now "commutes from Bloomington, Indiana to her post as full-time visiting professor of history at the University of Iowa."

Sometimes commuter couples respond that as far as sexual relationships go, "a weekend together doesn't make up for a month apart." This seems to be especially true in responses from blue collar and clerical couples. Some report that commuting has affected their sexual relationships adversely and a few report that it has cut off sex totally or at least from 90 to 99 percent. You can get some idea of the problems involved by considering the story that Marian and Robert tell.

"When Robert moved to Kearney to take a construction job with the power plant there, it cut off our sexual life almost totally. I wanted to stay in my new position here—I am just beginning to make important career advances as an administrative secretary. My schedule is more flexible than Robert's, so I drive there very weekend with Jamie, our 8-year-old daughter. Robert has rented a 26-foot travel trailer to live in. It was the best housing in Kearney he could find because of all the new industry there. With the three of us, with Jamie, in the trailer—there is no possible way. Occasionally she'll go off to play with a neighbor, but then, the whole trailer shakes. And Robert leveled it and shimmed it up as firmly as he could. Commuting cut off 99 percent of 'it' anyway."

So, clearly a commuter marriage is much more sexy if you have the money to make it so. It is like the old joke when you see an obvious artifact of affluence: the Mercedes-Benz, the gleaming white and chrome yacht, the Greek revival suburban mansion, the soft luxury of the fine fur coat, or whatever. You turn and look at each other and one of you asks, "But are they *really* happy?" The answer can only be "You'd better believe it!" Or at the very least, "It must be a very comfortable misery."

Another middle-income worker reported that her sexual relationship had been affected "very adversely" by commuting. Dorothy and Fred report that their commuter relationship is more of a necessity than a choice. It enables them to "pay our bills." In addition, Dorothy's family and friends were "shocked" when the couple made the decision to commute because they all felt she would not be able to cope with running a farm and her job all by herself (they live in a rural area and have a small acreage and a few animals). Instead of romantic interludes on weekends, the couple "work on all the projects that need two people to complete." During the week Dorothy keeps working on all the things that need to be done. She regrets having to make decisions when crises arrive without consulting with Fred. Her two teenage children do not pitch in but instead expect her to play a traditional housewife's role, cooking all meals, doing laundry, and generally being the family servant. What may be much more important and what may also have a profound influence on the unsatisfactory sexual relationship of the couple is Dorothy's report that it is her husband's career that comes first, "because he feels *he* has a 'career' and I'm only a 'secretary'."

Sexual Slavery

The notion of "sexual slavery" was proposed by Shere Hite in 1976. Hite wasn't talking about some new or even old kind of kinky relationship, or about sadomasochism. She was merely acknowledging the fact that the role of women in sex, as in every other aspect of life, has been to serve the needs of others—men and children. When the *Hite Report: A Nationwide Study of Female Sexuality* was published, women had become conscious of oppression in a general sense, but sexual slavery was still an unconscious way of life. Hite reported that women were justifiably afraid to "come out" with their own sexuality and were forced to satisfy others' needs while ignoring their own. Perhaps the idea is best expressed by one of the women in Hite's survey. She explained, "Sex can be political in the sense that it can involve a power structure where the woman is unwilling or unable to get what she really needs for her fullest amount of pleasure, but the man is getting what he wants, and the woman, like an unquestioning and unsuspecting lackey, is gratefully supplying it" (Hite 1976:281).

Women reported to Hite that they liked sex more for the feelings of closeness, the feeling of being needed and wanted, and the emotional warmth shared than for the purely physical sensations of intercourse. Hite proposes that although women know how to have orgasms, they are afraid to use this knowledge for fear of diminishing the closeness of sex.

In a dual-career, long-distance marriage, women indeed use their full sexual knowledge to break out of the pattern of foreplay, penetration, intercourse, and ejaculation because the three inhibiting factors proposed by Hite are absent.

Economics

Sexual exploitation and dissatisfaction have roots in powerlessness, not in lack of knowledge. Total dependency on the man with whom she has sex can bring economic intimidation, vulnerability, and a precarious position. In a traditional single-career family or in the dual-occupation family where the woman is seen merely as a cakewinner, a woman's position can be precarious because there are no economic alternatives that can provide food and shelter. Many traditional marriages are held together by a need to keep things financially secure. "After all, he does pay for everything."

Economically dependent wives put their husband's satisfaction before their own. They may want to please the man, but they don't feel at all free *not* to please him. Financial dependence doesn't put you in a good bargaining position to demand equality in bed. Only in extramarital affairs is there the freedom to say no that can make sex special and exciting. In a traditional marriage, affectionate words and embraces are sometimes merely powerful bartering tools.

Legally in marriage a woman *must* have intercourse with her husband. If you can't have sex, it's grounds for divorce or annulment; but love and affection are not required in a marriage. When women are no longer economically dependent, they don't always reevaluate their lifestyle or modify their sexual situation. But commuter marriage forces women, and men as well, to analyze their sexual needs. Because they are out from under the traditional role expectation and the traditional economic dependency, they are free to explore the possibility of becoming more than mere loving eunuchs. In the case of Dorothy and Fred described above, this never happened because Fred, in a highly traditional pattern, did not consider Dorothy's job as more than a meaningless fallback; and more important, she believed it. Economic problems were a large factor in this marriage, and Dorothy lacked social power, physical power, and economic power. With the sizzling couple, Dick and Jane, the situation was quite different. Respect for each other's individuality and successful careers seems to prompt an exotic, satisfying sex life.

Love

Shere Hite noted that it is remarkable how easily women bring themselves to orgasm during masturbation and how totally they ignore this knowledge during sex with men. Women have come to the point where they can demand equal pay, but a demand for equal sex is often considered invalid. To make the demand would be to risk losing men's "love." Women in dual-career marriages are no longer afraid to challenge men in bed for fear of losing love. Karen Barrett in *Ms.* says, "The relationship is strengthened when each partner is economically viable and feels that she or he is achieving a lot at work as well as at home" (1984:14). Women are challenging men every day in business and professional environments and find they can retain personal relationships without slavish obedience.

Sexual therapists have said that the frank reaching for sexual pleasure can cause fears of being abandoned. They relate some anxiety-producing ideas, such as the "fear of loss of love object," of women being "especially sensitive to potential separation from those with whom they have close relationships," etc. But this can be merely an example of the general cultural attitude transmitted to all women that indeed they cannot survive alone and are very likely to get into serious trouble if they are not supported by strong, capable males who protect them. Dorothy, the secretary, has received this message. She *needs* to consult with Fred before she can act on a decision. Her friends and relatives are "shocked" that she would try to go it alone.

Nevertheless, commuter couples have had to "bite the bullet" on the abandonment/loss of love issue. To put it simplistically, they are abandoned and have found that love can and does survive. Love is not physical proximity; it's much more. Jan Hodgson and James Bergfalk found this out. What sparks their romance is not fear of loss, but challenge and stimulation. And it's much better. The threats of potential desertion are found to be empty, and pressures for obedience to avoid desertion melt away. Commuters become full sexual persons, and the so-called "orgasm problem" fades.

The following, written by Alice Rossi in 1964 and frequently quoted, expresses the notion best.

If the view of the sex act presupposes a dominant male actor and a passive female subject, then it is indeed the case that full sex equality would probably be the death knell of this traditional sexual relationship. Men and women who participate as equals in their parental, occupational, and social roles will complement each other sexually in the same way, as essentially equal partners, and not as an ascendant male and a submissive female. This does not mean, however, that equality in non-sexual roles necessarily de-eroticized the sexual one. The enlarged base of shared experience can, if anything, heighten the salience of sex qua sex. The salience of sex may be enhanced precisely in the situation of the diminished significance of sex as a differentiating factor in all other areas of life. It has always seemed paradoxical to me that so many psychoanalysts defend the traditional sex roles and warn that drastic warping of the sexual impulses may flow from full sex equality; surely they are underestimating the power and force of the very drive which is so central a position in their theoretical framework. . . . [Maslow] found contrary to traditional notions of femininity and psychoanalytic theories, that the more "dominant" the woman, the greater her enjoyment of sexuality, the greater her ability to give herself freely in love. Women with dominance feelings were free to be completely themselves, and this was crucial for their full expression in sex. (Rossi 1964:648)

Habit

We are all taught what you are "spozed to do" with sex. We are taught that certain things are the proper physical relations between people, and these things are structured around the idea that sexual relations are a reproductive activity. This is all "spozed to be" instinctual, our nature. We're taught that our instincts make us have sex the way we do. But Shere Hite's research indicates that intercourse is not strictly natural. Sex and all physical relations are cultural forms. If they were not, we would not have all kinds of people from sex therapists to physicians to clergymen to men's and women's magazines instructing us in what sex is and in the proper way of "having it." They tell us when and where to touch, when to orgasm, that it's bad not to orgasm, that the male orgasm must take place, that females now must have multiple orgasms, and on, and on, and on. But they never seem to say that only we can know what we want at any given time, and that we can create sex in whatever image we want.

Standard definitions for everything are out for the commuting couple, who are engaged in a very nonstandard type of marriage. Therefore, they can more easily reject the standard definition of sex as foreplay, penetration, intercourse, and male ejaculation. Couples may no longer be afraid to use their knowledge during sex. Long-distance marriage lets people invent whatever kind of physical relations they want that seem natural at the time, depending upon their individual feelings and needs. This is why commuters can sometimes merely "cuddle together and sleep spoon fashion" or at other times enact the elaborate fantasies of "Dom Pérignon homecomings" and exotic, sexy nights with equal delight and satisfaction.

The ability to reject habit may be the most important aspect that contributes to the sexual pleasure of commuter couples. Commuters have already challenged standards and escaped traditional authority in their public lives because of their exotic lifestyle; so they see no reason to follow a mechanical pattern for being close to one another in their private lives.

The future of intercourse for the commuter couple looks very bright. Women have been tired of the old mechanical pattern of sexual relations which revolved around male erection, male penetration, and male orgasms for a long time. Men have become tired of the emphasis on performance and technique. Commuters seem to find more time, in less time, for tenderness, for touching, for gentleness, as well as for bare sexual stimulation. They see each other so seldom that they can avoid the mechanical concentration on perfection of performance. Knowing you *will* have intercourse is boring. If you know it has to be part of every encounter, it becomes mechanical. Commuters have un-defined their sexuality and have thus expanded their ideas of physical relationships to a new level of awareness. Sex seems to be generally more fun for them, but the full development of sexual awareness may be dependent upon the economic circumstances of the relationship. Sexual experience is enhanced by a positive concept of self. Women who are more dominant and whose positions are not demeaned by spouses seeking to protect their own self-esteem enjoy greater sexual fulfillment.

Dual-residence relationships don't have more sex, but the people involved enjoy sex more. Couples are generally highly monogamous and devoted to their sexual partners. The research evidence shows that the romantic sexual delights of long-distance marriage may be greater for couples with high incomes. Social problems, obstacles to privacy, and financial difficulties of commuter marriage at the lower income levels can diminish the "honeymoon" aspects. However, the couples who can use their imaginations in detailed planning of their "prime time" together have an advantage regardless of income level. It is really the care taken in shared time that is the important factor, and commuters seem to take more care because time is so precious.

Chapter Four

"Let No Man Put Asunder!"
Social Taboos

"**M**y new life seems to make people uneasy. They don't know what sexual label to put on me—married, divorced, or available?" says a commuting professor of English in New Mexico. A male Proctor and Gamble executive says, "I don't see how anyone would want to do that. If you're married, you're supposed to be together." The demands of work regulate our activities and basic family social unit; yet the myth that the family organizes our activities continues to dominate and is responsible for the frequently negative responses of friends and family to commuter marriage.

The classic reaction to commuter marriage is, "When are you getting the divorce?" The unique arrangement of a long-distance marriage is viewed by others as a stage in marital breakdown. Real estate agents are suddenly on your doorstep asking if they can list your property for sale. When asked why they think it might be available, the answer is usually, "Uh, well, uh, I heard that you and your wife were no longer living together and, so, uh, I assumed. . . ."

The two-city marriage breaks a rigid moral commitment to the traditional family. Because this new social structure demonstrates that the major concern in our culture is not the family, nor intimacy, but work, it breaks very powerful taboos. Friends, relatives, and even our own children have difficulty accepting this new lifestyle. Evelyn Goodrick expressed the reaction most clearly when she wrote in *McCall's*:

This odd-couple arrangement has come about because of our jobs. Our oldest daughter, a senior in college, who is usually not at a loss for words, admits she has trouble explaining the situation to friends. Our youngest daughter giggles and says people don't understand—they think her parents are divorced, or something conventional like that. Our middle daughter, who is 18, doesn't like to joke about it at all. She finds it embarrassing that her mother has left home for a job. (Goodrick 1980:68)

The daughter in this instance finds the situation embarrassing because a cultural taboo has been broken, and the sky has not fallen in. Evelyn Goodrick is happy. She has a job that she can smile about, a husband who is completely supportive, and confidence in a relationship that did not require constant "togetherness." But breaking taboos as Evelyn did requires courage. It is an act of power.

The two-city relationship also breaks the cultural commitment to insure the male's freedom to work while the female assumes responsibility for the domestic domain. This cultural commitment to the male work force is kept in place by an occupational system which in practice has generally excluded women from most high-status jobs. The exclusion of women is justified on the assumption of women's higher emotional investment in the family and their supposedly lower occupational commitment. The situation becomes the classic self-fulfilling prophecy. Women, excluded from fulfilling work, and having instead sought fulfillment through their families and care-giving, can not then take back their investment. It is a part of the unwritten marriage contract, and it works both ways because it also excludes males from care-giving contact with children. Once committed to the work force, men can not take back their investment and seek fulfilling contact within the home.

Commuter marriage blurs the barriers between work and care-giving. That is, neither partner can undertake only one role, but must assume both the domestic and the work role. The work and home environments are more compartmentalized than in a single home, dual-career situation, but each partner must assume both domestic and work roles for a portion of the week. Although this has advantages from the standpoint of hours that may be devoted to work and career advancement, it also has disadvantages because society has not yet learned to accept the married-single lifestyle, and a social support system is lacking. "Friends thought it could be the beginning of the end of our marriage," said a 35-year-old commuting wife who had been married for seventeen years. She was relating the almost universal negative response that commuters receive from outsiders.

Five major social dilemmas exist for the commuter couple. Each dilemma can be clearly seen in biographical information from commuter couples, but all couples develop some means of coping with and resolving these dilemmas.

The "Hester Prynne Response"

In other words, whither he goest, I go, too. Or did. When I finally abandoned that code, along with a surefire convenient job, I didn't receive much emotional support other than from Dick, my husband. My mother, who was employed for years, still tells me, "I would never have left my children." Others ask, "How is the job going?" as if waiting for news of some disaster. (Goodrick 1980:68)

Friends, employers, extended family, in fact, all significant others attempt to impose their definitions of marriage on the commuting couple. When the couple rejects these expectations, others propose that there is something wrong with the marriage. There is a clash between personal norms, the behavior that commuting couples feel is right for them, and social norms, the behavior that people around them expect the couple to conform to. The Hester Prynne dilemma arises for wives because most women would never leave a husband and family to pursue a career. Instead they would give up a career to become a "trailing spouse." Commuter wives don't wear the visible scarlet letter of Hester Prynne, but they do receive the same censuring responses from others. They are condemned by society because they break the hidden contracts of both work and marriage. An

employer said of two-city marriage, "I can't understand why anyone would want to do that—it just isn't natural."

The commuter spouse is considered deviant even by
close family members. "My mother was shocked and other relatives said of my husband 'Oh he's going off and leaving you
again.' I was the one who didn't want to go—my business was
just getting started," said a microcomputer vendor. A professor
of psychology said, "My relatives only accepted it after they
thought it was stable. By then we'd been commuting for three
years." "My friends said, 'Wow! That must be hard. How do you
do it? Bet you can't wait until you're together.'" The outside
world looks at commuter couples critically, and the target of
most of the criticism is the women. Women have been the last
to come into their own, and so they are the first to be criticized.
Their rapidly changing status makes them vulnerable because
powerful social rules in this country state that the wife must
subordinate her ambition to her husband's and that a couple
must live together to be considered married.

Because there is always the underlying suspicion on the
part of mutual friends that the marriage is on the rocks, the
female married single is often left out of networks with other
married couples. A 35-year-old commuting wife who had been
married for fifteen years reported, "Friends thought it could be
the beginning of the end of our marriage." But the married-
single commuter isn't divorced or even divorcing; so there is no
access to the usual singles' networks or other support systems
for people who are indeed separated.

Advisers and psychologists are not much help either. One
couple described in *Money* (Lavoie 1977:85) was told to "close
the gap, or suffer the consequences," the consequences being
failure of the marriage. "The first thing to do is to organize your
family life. If you don't, your assets will eventually go to build up
the portfolios of two dear, sweet, kindly divorce lawyers," said
Robert Waill, an economist, while a lawyer and an executive
recruiter concurred completely. None of the three advisers considered that living together, apart, was good even though it
allowed the couple to achieve their goal of seeing their elderly
Russian parents through a comfortable old age. None consid-

ered that the traditional Russian cultural beliefs the couple held made living together, apart, far from a sacrifice. Anything other than sleeping together each night in the same bed is considered "unnatural" by most family experts. Articles read, "long-distance marriage raises many an eyebrow among co-workers, friends, and relatives" (Lavoie 1977:76), and these raised eyebrows are an enormously inhibiting factor in trying to successfully manage two careers and an intimate relationship.

The "Unmacho Response"

Conventional guidelines implanted in early socialization say, "There's something unmacho about going where your wife goes . . . it needs lots of explaining." But allowing your wife to go in the first place is equally reprehensible. A husband can no longer assume his wife's automatic commitment to providing domestic backup services for his career. He can't assume she'll pick up and move, taking whatever position she can get in the new location. Men say: "It's hard for a man to tell his employers he can't move unless his spouse or girlfriend gives her approval." A lawyer in Phoenix says, "Commuting is fine, but the problem comes when I'm on her turf. Being dependent on your partner in her lair is a threat." Another husband said to Dick Friedman in *Working Woman* that he was afraid of becoming the victim if he moved with his wife. "Ok, so I move for her job. What's going to happen to *me*? What if I can't find a new job? or, what if I find a job but it's not as good as my old one, or I end up taking a whopping salary cut—what will that do to my ego?" (1981:18).

When a woman says she can't move without a husband's approval, she gets a wide range of opinions from friends, family, and co-workers. They tell her to either move, stay here, get rid of the bum, or equally creative suggestions. Men, however, get one opinion. "It is unmanly to have a wife refuse to be a trailing spouse." Something must be lacking in the relationship, and what is lacking is generally assumed to be sexual prowess. Sociologists Kirschner and Walum (1978) propose that it is much more difficult for the male than for the female of the couple to find a support system. Their discussion of the difficulties encountered by male commuters expresses what the majority of husbands interviewed felt.

> *Men may be viewed as weak because they are "allowing" their wives to be away, or they are viewed as having the best of two worlds because they are somehow managing to be both bachelors and married at the same time. It is interesting to note that in the historical examples given [military, immigrants, salesmen, executives], the males who established two-location families most often did so inside supportive systems. For example, military units are strongly bonded, immigrants often came to this country either in kinship or village groups and/or joined members of these groups already established in this country. . . .*
>
> *The modern day two-location family frequently deprives the male of his already established support system, the nuclear family, and does not provide any structural substitute. Extended family frequently denegrate his manliness. Close friends of the couple may "drop" the single male. Male culture is not supportive of or sympathetic to the male who "lets" his wife go off on her own, and especially not so if she has left him with the children. As one informant suggested, watching a sports event with the guys in the local bar is the nearest he could get to a male support group, and they were not very supportive. These men, he commented, assumed he was going to swing all night while they had to check in with their wives. (Kirschner and Walum 1978:522)*

When a husband is left with the children, the situation is doubly difficult. One father reports that the admiring, congratulatory remarks of the other "mothers" when they meet him delivering his daughter to school or in the supermarket are a trial. "Why should it be something special, something to be considered strange? I took the kids to school before we began commuting. Can't I become involved in the care of my children without being considered a weirdo?"

Serious careers have required and needed the second person. In a commuter arrangement, you have no one there to back you up. Career politics become difficult to manage. This is especially noticeable for males who operate under the game rules designed by men that are married to second persons. The idea of two first persons simply hasn't been around very long. Men begin to notice the loss of the second person in small, but annoying, situations. Usually it's a spur-of-the-moment situation. Scott tells about how it happened to him. "My boss called down and asked if I could fly to Brussels on a rush situation that might open new markets for the company. Naturally, I agreed, but then I couldn't find my new electric shaver and I only had one clean shirt in the closet. The shaver was in Boulder where Mary Jane lives, and I'd forgotten to get the shirts to the laundry. Frankly, I was resentful. Why should I, a corporate executive, have to see to my own laundry? And worse yet, Mary Jane wasn't even around to see how damned mad I was."

Career rule number one says that the first person doesn't have to worry about the logistics of food, laundry, clothing, shelter, or other necessary items while working. These are as available as beer at a ballgame. Dirty clothes are automatically picked up, cleaned, pressed, and hung up. Meals are served whenever the first person is hungry. Only maintenance chores requiring the actual physical presence of the first person require time: things like visits to barbers, doctors, lawyers, or civic duties such as voting.

Career rule number two says that the first person must be ready to work whenever and wherever it is best for career advancement, and career rule number three says that the first person has a cheering section at home (Bird 1979). Commuter marriage breaks all three of these rules, and it is most difficult for the male because historically men expect these things as part of their rights, as the "normal" prerogatives of the career game player.

Conflicts Between Marital and Work Roles

"The big problem is that both of us need a wife," said not one, but many commuting couples. Two-city marriage is subject to conflict between domestic expectations and work expectations. Commuting couples are very busy people who are committed to their demanding occupations. In addition, they have each other and possibly growing children that they value very highly, and this creates another demanding situation. Because of time constraints, couples tend to have a less active involvement with extended family and fewer friendships. Right now, not in some futuristic twenty-first century, there are enough women earning enough money outside their homes to break forever the "What will the Joneses say?" pathway through life that is based on the assumption that all men ought to be breadwinning husbands and all women ought to be homemaking wives and mothers.

During the seventies women entered the job market at an increasing rate. The conventional pattern of the American homemaker was over. Of course, most of these women were untrained. They were like immigrant workers, rural farmers moving to the cities, sharecroppers, wetbacks. They took the bottom-level jobs and sought positions that wouldn't interfere with their families. Now, instead of children keeping women at home, children are forcing women to work. It is simply too costly to stay home when children need clothes and college, when you need a new car, when you want to buy a house. Women were working to "help out," but everyone had in mind a standard of living that required more and more consumer goods, and a temporary situation became a permanent one.

At first these "pink collar" workers were very careful not to interrupt the traditional marriage-contract rules making wives responsible for domestic support. Practically no one noticed that they were away from home. Even today women are largely responsible for household upkeep, cooking, laundry, child care, and other services in single-residence, dual-paycheck households. But gradually this has been changing. And it has changed much more rapidly for commuter couples. Commuter couples face the housework dilemma of "who does what" just as any other two-career family does, but they have to face it in two locations. Because of the compartmentalized lifestyle, commuters can avoid much of the who-does-what hassle. "We pretty much each take care of our own places," says Marjorie, a 32-year-old engineer who does the Phoenix–San Diego flight each weekend. "Where we get into difficulty is in executive housekeeper tasks—neither of us seems to do them, so we never have dental appointments, medical checkups, or balanced checkbooks. Frequently, we run through the whole series of warnings on overdue bills before we realize neither of us has paid." Ray, Marjorie's photographer husband, responds, "We're lax on those things, but we're not lax when it comes to our work. Self-fulfillment in our work seems more important. Luckily I don't work for a large corporation and my hours are flexible. I find I put in 16 or 18 hours a day sometimes, but I don't need a spouse at my side to be a hostess for corporate functions."

While relatives, friends, and counselors view commuting couples with raised eyebrows and suggestions of doom, business views them as the potential loss of the two-person, single-career benefit that has been traditionally available. It is an advantage to organizations to have employees who can devote their total energies to work roles without having to cope with the support needed for daily living. What can you do if 8-year-old Billy suddenly develops a fever in the middle of the school day? Who will pick him up if there is no wife at home? Are you actually willing to plow through the supermarket after 11 P.M. when you've put in a 14-hour day? Companies are working on solutions to the problems of dual-career couples and for solutions to relocation questions that make dual-residence marriage more and more frequent. For the moment, however, there are no easy answers, and many might agree with William Chafe, a professor at Duke University and a student of the American family, who states in the *Wall Street Journal*, "Couples who want to have both dual-career and children will never make it to the top of their professions. It's tough enough to do it in the first place, but it can never be done in this situation. Childless couples will have an easier time of it, but not without sacrifices, such as weekend commuting if a transfer is crucial to a career" (Gallese 1978:1).

Cultural Conceptions of Child Rearing

Childless couples clearly have an advantage in the two-location relationship because they avoid some of the most serious conflicts, caused by cultural expectations of what good mothers and fathers should be. What does society expect of parents, and what do we believe about children? Experts have told us some of the following things that have made a great impact upon the way you feel when you decide to live together, apart. Briefly these guilt-producing conceptions are as follows:

1. Children's needs take precedence over adult needs because the child is society's most valuable resource.
2. The first few years are critical because child care involves more than feeding, shelter, and physical needs. This is the time when children are given experience that will be the basis for a healthy personality. (Recent evidence seriously questions this position.)
3. Good mothering requires the constant presence of the mother, especially in the early experience. (Outrage is appropriate from all nonmaternal child care providers.)
4. The father is only indirectly important as a protector and provider for the mother-child couplet. (Outrage is appropriate from all fathers, especially single ones.)
5. Parents who had good parenting know how to be good parents, but parents who did not, do not.
6. Being a good parent comes naturally. (A clear contradiction of the above!)
7. The mother-child bond is biologically determined and is best for long-term trials of parenthood. (Outrage is appropriate from all caretakers of children who are not "biological mothers.")
8. Mothers' needs and infants' needs are complementary. (Disbelief is appropriate from all working mothers.)
9. Parenting involves sacrifice, but the rewards balance the sacrifices.
10. No compromises are possible with the *totality* of dedication that is required.

These ten misconceptions are adapted from the writing of Rhonda and Robert Rapoport (1977:35–36), who are two of the early experts on dual-career marriage. The writers note that the conceptions were derived from psychoanalytic writing, medical care givers' advice, the social sciences, the legal system, and educational institutions. They note that these assumptions about parenting have altered, but that many of them still prevail. The Rapoports suggest these authoritative formulations disallow diversity and cause stress for nontraditional families who seek to conform to the expectation of the "normal," "mature" male as economic provider and the "normal," "mature" female as a mother. It is beyond the scope of this book to refute the guilt-producing conceptions listed above, but should you be having difficulty with dilemmas from child-rearing expectations, it would be well worth reading *American Couples* (Blumstein and Schwartz 1983) to see what actually happens in day-to-day life for thousands of couples. The "parents are people too" perspective relieves the feeling of "I'm sure we're doing it all wrong; so we'll suffer the consequences later."

At least be assured that you are not the only commuter feeling this way. It even happens to commuting child psychologists. Famous ones at that. John Meier commuted between Denver and Washington for almost two years while he was head of the Office of Child Development and chief of the Children's Bureau in the Department of Health, Education, and Welfare between 1975 and 1977. His three daughters, then aged 8, 11, and 13, remained at home with their mother. Meier reported to an interviewer that "when his older daughter learned that he was taking a job dealing with child abuse and neglect she asked him, 'What about neglecting your own children?'" The Meiers believe, as do many, that absence can have a negative impact on children. Neither would recommend commuting as a permanent arrangement when you have kids. But not everyone agrees. Lester Hyman, a Washington, D.C., attorney, and his wife Helen plan to continue commuting indefinitely despite their three children, aged 17, 15, and 12. Helen Hyman went back to law school several years ago, and when she graduated she opened a small-town practice in the Berkshires, where they had previously had a summer home. Lester says, "We had a family powwow to talk things over. The kids were willing to try it, and it has worked out beautifully." Helen believes that it can only be done with children if you have a strong marriage—or no marriage at all. "I like to think that mine is in the former category" (U.S. *News and World Report* 1977:110).

About one-third of all commuter couples interviewed had children. Rhodes and Rhodes (1984), however, report that half of two-city families include children and face the value conflicts between care-giving and self-actualization. One commuter who managed a parking garage and auto repair business in Greenville, N.C., said he didn't believe his wife's move to Washington would be good for their children, two boys aged 4 and 9. The boys are staying with their father, and he says, "The kids are very attached to her. This move isn't good for them, it's only good for her." Some couples find that their children thrive and grow more responsible and cooperative as they have to begin to share more in maintaining the family unit. Others feel they are being cut out of the family unit when children become dependent on the partner who is the major caretaker. One wife remembers vividly the hurt she felt when her baby cried because she didn't know her.

The one factor that most couples seemed to emphasize as necessary for success in the long-distance arrangement with children was the absolute need for the children to understand the situation. They need to know that you're not separating for lack of love and mutual respect, but because of it. "They need to know that your work is important to you, that it is a part of your self-respect and your very being. They also have to understand that your commitment to your work in no way diminishes your feelings for them. It's not easy to achieve this, but it's necessary. Especially the fears they may have about divorce," said an Atlanta commuter.

Business Week (1978) tells an interesting story about children's concepts of commuter couples. Although many couples like to wait until their children are in their teens before beginning two households, Joe A. Kelly relates that his daughter Debra, who is 18, was a commuter child from almost the beginning. Maxine Kelly is vice president of Monet Jewelers Inc. and commutes on weekends from New York to Houston, where Joe is a semiretired aeronautical engineer. The couple relate that years ago Debra asked a playmate: "When does *your* Mommy go to New York?" Maxine is confident that "When children are raised in a certain situation, they don't always realize that others are any different." The moral of the story, of course, is that you may be doing too much worrying and feeling too much guilt about how your lifestyle will affect your children. If you feel good about yourself, the children will most certainly thrive. The Rapoports (1977:361) offer the following hints for new directions in parenting that you might want to explore.

Sharing of Parenting. Experience different patterns of parental division of labor. What are the satisfactions and the impediments?

Broaden the Concept of Parenting. Include supplementary figures other than mothers and fathers both inside and outside the family, such as: children, kin, professional helpers, friends. What are their potentials, and what are the drawbacks?

Alternative Parenting Arrangements Camps, communes, intimate networks, and informal fostering could be possibilities, as well as letting older teens try it on their own.

When you're torn by the care-giving, self-actualization dilemma, keep in mind that parents have rights too. Parenting is only one set of interests that you have among many. The place of parenthood in people's lives is being reevaluated, and people now feel there should be a balance within families. Other involvements besides family are important, and the needs of parents and the needs of children do *not* always coincide. The best you can hope for is an arrangement that will have a mixture so that neither will unduly suffer. Biological parents are not the only people who should be involved in parenting. Most cultures realized this long ago and have made other arrangements. Parenting consists of too many elements for a mother or even a father to meet all needs. What seems to be the top thing to keep in mind is that there are many, many ways of being a "good parent." There is no single correct set of parenting roles to follow. If there were, everyone would to it perfectly. As a person you have unique capabilities that you will bring with you to the parenting game. Use them. No matter what you do, parenting is a dilemma because there is no perfect solution and the result may be different from what you would desire. Not even the *best* principles of child care can guarantee perfect success; there are far too many factors. What is right for one child may be totally wrong for another.

Unconventional Intimacy Relationships

Berger and Keller (1964:1) speak of marriage as a social arrangement that creates the sort of order in which individuals can experience life as making sense. That is, the close social relationship occurring in face-to-face situations on a day-to-day basis are given primary significance by a couple and in turn give reality to the world and sustain the reality of the marriage. The question is, are other modes of interaction, such as the telephone or the exchange of letters, sufficient to sustain the relationship? Historically, many couples seemed to thrive on letter-writing. Published examples would include the letters of Elizabeth Barrett Browning and Robert Browning or those of Abigail and John Adams. Today commuters may not publish their letters—as yet—but they frequently report they are using this means of communication more often, and that they enjoy it. Some say seeing the familiar handwriting in the mailbox on returning from a difficult day is almost as comforting as a homecoming embrace. "I used to save Larry's letters until I'd returned from my three-mile run, showered, and had my dinner going. Then I'd sit down with a cup of tea and it was almost as if we were together. I could hear Larry's voice, but it was better than his voice because it was permanent. I'd read certain passages over and over," says Maria. With rapid changes occurring in telehone communications, it may not be long before voice-to-voice sharing will be less costly. Satellite communications now being installed by many major organizations could make it possible to use the phone as habitually as we now have a cup of coffee. Telephones are the major tool used by two-city couples to ward off loneliness and maintain their intimacy. It seems strange to insist that face-to-face interaction is necessary to maintain the reality of a marriage and give reality and order to the world.

Instead, there is the question of whether continual face-to-face interaction leads to greater intimacy at all. It is questionable whether any adult can bear total immersion in a relationship, except for brief periods. What too often happens with day-to-day routines is the erosion of the intensity of the relationship. Interactions begin to consist of dealing with the mundane details of life. If familiarity doesn't lead to contempt, it can certainly lead to boredom. Retirement is a good example. One of the most difficult problems for retired couples is the increased daily interaction when a spouse retires. Wives will often say, "I wish he'd get out from under my feet," or "I can never be alone anymore." One might speculate that knowing that the amount of time a couple has to spend together is limited can lead to more intense intimacy rather than increasing loneliness. However, it is not the husband and wife alone who create their reality. If it were, the long-distance situation might be easier to live with.

To maintain the reality of marriage imposed on couples by extended family, friends, and employers, 99 percent of the couples who live together, apart, resort to the strategy of insisting that they are "only doing this temporarily." They report, "We're giving ourselves two years to get together," or "It's only temporary. Henry is looking for a job near here." This attitude is so common that *Time* suggests that "commuters single-mindedly await the day when they can become ordinary one-city folk again. 'They are functioning on "deferred gratification,"' says sociologist Sussman. They are, in other words, the new troops of the Protestant ethic, enduring hardship now for the sake of better days ahead" (Leo 1982:84).

Or are they? Must better days be days when they reside together on a day-to-day basis? Perhaps it is only cultural expectations that give this impression. Commuters may merely be playing by the rules of what is expected of "normal" marriage. The required behavior, at least for the moment, is that a couple live together. If you can't do that because of a career considerations, you must at the very least say that you would *like* to do it. That it is the ideal. But is it? Commuters may, beneath the facade, have other ideas that would be considered so unconventional they hesitate to admit these notions even to each other.

The truth is, there are many patterns of marriage, and it is impossible to prescribe one for all couples. What seems the right sort of intimacy relationship for one couple may be strange and stressful for another. Charles Handy (1978:36–46), professor of Management Development at the London Graduate School of Business and a specialist in the education of managers and the design of organizations, explored and plotted definable marriage patterns. He was looking at four dimensions based upon expressed attitudes or dispositions of the 23 couples involved in his research: achievement, dominance, affiliation, and nurturance. Handy plotted the results of scores to form a matrix of four quadrants, and titles were given to each section, as in the diagram.

Patterns of Marriage

Achievement,
Dominance

	High	**A** INVOLVED	**B** THRUSTING
	Low	**D** SUPPORTIVE	**C** LONERS
		High	Low

Affiliation,
Nurturance

SOURCE: Adapted from Handy (1978:38)

In Quadrant A are people designated as "involved." These people have high needs to achieve and to dominate, but they also have a desire for a strong intimate relationship, since they score highly on the affiliation-nurturance dimension.

Quadrant B people were called "thrusting" by Handy. They are the high achievers with a need for dominance but with less sensitivity to group or intimate relationships. Handy found that this quadrant contained the most visibly successful males.

The lower-right Quadrant C contains the loners, or what Handy calls "existentialists." They have little desire to control others or to look after others. They are inner-directed, set their own standards, and are not considered ambitious by usual standards.

In the lower-left Quadrant D are the supportive, caring people who enjoy looking after others and belonging, rather than dominating. Handy found that many executives' wives fell into this quadrant, but only 2 men in the 23 couples Handy studied.

To arrive at marriage patterns, Handy combined the husbands' orientation with the wives'; that is, a thrusting man might be married to a supportive wife (the stereotypical B-D pattern), or a supportive husband could theoretically be married to a thrusting wife (a more unusual D-B pattern). There are 16 possible patterns. However, with Handy's restricted sample, selected from male career executives in large organizations who were in an advanced management training program, only 8 of the possiblilities were represented. His 23 couples included only 4 that could be described as true working couples, but the interesting fact is that *none* of the working couples were found in the stereotypical thrusting male–supportive wife B-D pattern, even though it *was* the most commonly occurring pattern of husband-wife interaction at the managerial level.

What are the implications for maintaining intimacy in these possible interactional patterns for dual-career couples, and what would be the interactional pattern of couples who take their work situations so seriously as to decide to undertake a commuter marriage? To see how interaction differs with these unusual couples it is best to look first at the conventional stereotyped B-D pattern.

Thruster-supportive or B-D couples have as a common goal his achievement and his success outside the home. She concentrates on the home, on the children (who are well disciplined), and on keeping him happy. Role conceptions are clear, and each partner knows exactly what is expected. The wife is supportive of her husband at work, but she shows little or no interest in the details. Handy reports that one wife, a highly supportive one, did not in fact know what her husband's job was, although she did know the name of his employers. Supportive wives will readily move if the husband's work demands it. Homes are neat and tidy, and there are usually separate activities prescribed for each room. Commonly there will be a particular room set aside for the husband as a den or study.

Two aspects of interaction that clearly differentiate couples' patterns of intimacy are language use and responses to stress. The language of the typical B-D, thrusting-supportive, couples tends to be ritualistic and logistic. For example, "How was the office today?" or "When are the Roberts coming over for dinner?" There are few issue-raising comments, such as, "I read that Virginia Harris, the president of the Federal Bank, has been turned down for membership in your Union Club." In the absence of discussions of issues, there are also few conflicts. When conflicts do arise, the thrusting male turns the stress into physical rituals (sports, gardening, hunting) or back into his work, while the supportive wife tries not to express her tensions and suffers in silence and solitude to "protect" the family from unpleasantness. Conflicts and stresses are not discussed, since conversational rituals don't allow for it. The key word is harmony, peace at any price, and although this may sound dull, a man fully involved in work may feel comfortable with this type of intimacy rather than with a turbulent relationship with another thruster.

Handy found that working couples fell into three interactional patterns, but the B-B pattern, thruster husband and thruster wife, was the most common. Both partners here want achievement and dominance. Both want an arena where they can have responsibility and demonstrate their expertise by achievement. Part-time work and courses of study or hobbies are inadequate for these thruster wives. A high degree of planning and organization is needed to cope with the logistic support problems of the family, since neither partner is strong on the "order" dimension but would prefer a supportive second person to organize the domestic base. Home life can become downright chaotic, and both find this irritating. Tensions then arise if the husband seeks to blame the wife, pushing the supportive-caring role upon her. At worst, since thrusting people tend to become aggressive under stress, the spouses may move against each other and clash in recriminatory arguments.

If you find that you would probably place yourself and your spouse in Quadrant B, commuter marriage may indeed be an ideal situation for you—even over the long haul. Commuter couples with the B-B interaction pattern are apt to say of their relationship, "Our particular positions are more important to us than each other at this point," and then conclude that "This is a miserable statement." However, it may not be a miserable statement at all. If there are equal opportunities outside the home, the intimacy relationship can be extremely supportive for both partners, since the strong interests that allow you to stimulate each other can then be maintained. Should the thrusting wife decide to become the trailing spouse in the traditional pattern, intimacy could easily turn to resentment. It would seem better to seek the unconventional arrangement of a long-distance relationship where you both can find separate activities, have romantic homecomings, and develop a stable, contented relationship.

The marriage of two "involved" people, the A-A pattern of interaction, also involves two dominant high-achievers, but in this case attitudes are tempered, or as Handy suggests, confused, by the high value each places on caring and belonging. Since these couples prefer to share arenas, not separate them, their marriages are role-overlapping. There are few clear duties. Whoever is available cooks, cleans, or puts the children to bed. Rooms are used for multiple purposes, and housework takes a low priority. Children are often full family members and seem to outsiders to be undisciplined. Conversations are quite different from those of the traditional B-D couples. Two involved partners talk more about issues than about logistics. But tensions can be high in these marriages, largely because both partners are sensitive and caring and yet they have rejected traditional guidelines of behavior. Under stress the couple will first withdraw and then move *toward* each other, where they talk things out for long hours.

The decision to undertake a two-city marriage is a hard one for two people with an A-A (involved-involved) intimacy pattern, much harder than for the B-B thruster couples. First of all, their social networks tend to be shared when they live in a single residence but lost almost entirely when the long-distance arrangement is undertaken. While the Hester Prynne Response or Unmacho Response might not bother the two thrusters, the involved partners are sensitive to becoming pariahs within their social network. These are the couples who must maintain the notion that their commuter marriage is merely a temporary arrangement. And indeed, for them it may be only temporary. Since both partners place high value on caring and belonging, they both have a greater tolerance for assuming the role of trailing spouse should it in the last instance become necessary. To sustain the belief that the commuter situation is temporary, these couples will consider one home as their primary residence and the other as a sort of satellite. Spouses designate the place where they generally reunite as "home," or "our home," while the secondary residence is sometimes called "my house," or "my apartment." Thruster couples would rarely make this subtle language distinction. They would more generally consider both residences as primary and talk about "my home" or "Roger's home." Thrusters who commute use first person singular pronouns (I, my, me) or third person pronouns (he/she, his/hers, him/her), but two involved people will more frequently use the first person plural pronouns (we, our, us). Two people whose intimacy relationship is based upon an involved interaction can be successful in a commuter marriage arrangement because the high value placed upon caring and support increases their tolerance for a situation which is in some respects antithetical to their needs and values.

Commuter couples more than likely would not have an interactional pattern of A-D, an involved husband with a supportive wife. This pattern goes less against the social grain. His work is accepted as important, and the wife's priority is accepted as supportive. The roles may be less clear-cut, since he is involved or caring, but where the wife works in these relationships, the work is generally of low importance and frequently part-time. It is undertaken by the supportive wife with the motivation to earn extra money temporarily or to provide companionship for herself if there are no children. But in situations of prolonged economic crisis, this type of interaction could move to a dual-occupation level and possibly in time to a dual-career, single-residence marriage.

Although Handy found no working couples with the C-C pattern, where both are loners, the pattern might be possible in situations of two artists, writers, or other people engaged in solitary uncompetitive activities. Two loners might undertake a relationship to use a common, domestic situation, but there would actually be little interaction. It would seem highly unlikely that the C-C pattern would be an interactional pattern found among commuter couples, since the individuals would lack the two factors that produce a long-distance marriage in the first place: commitment to a career and high commitment to each other.

Most people close to a commuter couple, especially employers and extended family, would like to see a more conventional pattern of intimacy. This pressure sometimes forces dual-career couples to reject the option of living together, apart, which might be a more viable alternative than career sacrifice. Until the social support system is ready to accept newer patterns of intimacy as real and normal rather than as deviant or neurotic, the commuter couple will be faced with the dilemma of resolving personal intimacy needs in the direction that the broader culture sees as necessary for a marital relationship.

A Social Support System for Commuter Marriage

"Some other aspects of their marriage have changed too. When they are together now, George and Janet have less time for their mutual friends. Each of the spouses has a tendency to develop their own circle of friends" (Nichols 1978:54). Since the first real public notice was taken of long-distance marriage in newspaper and magazine articles in 1977, there has been a gradual change in tone. By 1984 there was more emphasis on "making it work" than on "closing the gap." But until there is broader acceptance of this new social structure, what do couples do to contend with the Hester Prynne Response and the Unmacho Response? Most couples speak largely about mutual understanding and support as being critical. That is, they encourage each other despite negative responses from the outside. "He thinks our being married should not infringe on my career, and he keeps reminding me of that by telling me so," said one wife. Social life for couples changes, however. Some might say it suffers, because there is little time left for outsiders. A husband in San Jose, California, says, "We used to see a lot of friends on weekends and do a lot of entertaining. Now we have almost cut off outsiders—there's not much time and it's easier to just be together and not have to explain things."

Commuters have almost no time for mutual friends, but their support system can more easily develop through encouraging separate circles of friends in the two locations where they live. Shirley Young, executive vice president of Grey Advertising in New York who commutes to Detroit on weekends, resisted the temptation to isolate herself from criticism and from others in the ambiguous status as a married single. She reports:

Initially I felt uncomfortable as a single. . . . I wouldn't go to parties, but then I realized that people wanted to see me and didn't require me to have an escort. Now I call a friend if I need someone for a dinner dance, or my husband comes in for special events. Certainly there are advantages. I've freed myself of a stereotypical way of life—it's great to work late and not feel guilty. (Cecere 1983:139)

With spouses finding themselves as married singles, they are unable to produce a husband or wife for business obligations and family events, but adjustments are made. Self-imposed isolation is something that a commuter has to watch out for, but for women there is an advantage. Because of the women's movement of the past two decades, there are well-established women's groups and a developing tradition of mutual support. The networks created by feminist interest groups can in some measure make up for the lack of a social network composed of kin, friends, and neighbors. This type of network support is not so readily available to males, whose networks might be limited by their commuter travel to work associates or the good old boys in the cocktail lounge.

Another aspect of social networks is the quality of the relationship involved. As well as the sheer quantity of social relationships, dimensions such as depth of the support system are important. Overall, commuting couples report fewer social contacts because of their ambiguous social status, but they seem to be only slightly disturbed by this. One said, "We each have a few devoted friends in our separate cities. That and our relationship is enough."

But we are at a pivotal point in history. Two views of work exist simultaneously. For some people, even in advanced societies, work remains a necessary evil, something to be endured, or something to which you can become accustomed. For others, especially the highly qualified, it is an area within which they receive their major satisfactions—frequently satisfactions that are superior to those of other spheres of their lives, such as family life, leisure, or participation in community activities. Michael Fogarty (1971:33) noted that work may even incorporate elements traditionally considered separate. In a postindustrial society, the society which has now arrived with computer technology, work offers a growing scope of possibilities for personal development and fulfillment. The nature of work in the United States is evolving from a muscle economy to a brain economy. Industry is based more on service than on smokestacks, and along with this there is a subtle shift in what is required for work and for leadership. Sensitivity and creativity become important. A balance is now being achieved in the workplace between teamwork and individual effort, between autonomous work groups and central direction, and between "network" management (patterns) and bureaucracy. Eli Ginzberg, a Columbia University sociologist, suggests that we are entering an era when the dual-income family may become the most important social change of the twentieth century. The long-term implications of this are uncharted, but it seems likely that traditional marriage should and will eventually be redefined.

A small but growing group of counselors and advisers are rejecting the idea that long-distance marriage must necessarily lead to problems. They are accepting it as a viable alternative to career sacrifice, but feel that the commuter marriage partners need to develop a support system where they are living.

Usually, social support systems for people engaged in unconventional lifestyles are developed by interaction with others in the same unconventional situations. Most dual-career couples relate socially with others who are also dual-career couples. Generally couples who are trying out alternative work patterns such as flexitime, job-sharing, or job-alternating find other couples involved in the same work patterns. This allows the sharing of experiences, ideas, solutions, and most of all support. But commuter couples have a serious drawback in establishing contact with other commuters—time! With a 10- to 12-hour work day, plus travel to another city on weekends, there is less time for mutual friends. Leisure time is no problem for them because it doesn't exist. It is spent commuting. In addition, the unique arrangement of two-city families makes it necessary that social relations be limited to others who are not likely to be threatened by innovative lifestyles. Commuters, because of the negative response of others, are frequently almost secretive about their living together, apart, arrangement. Everyone has heard about them, but they have to be found through the grapevine. It seems there are many "closet commuters" at the moment, and therefore the lifestyle has few structural or cultural supports. Couples are cautious but positive when asked if they would recommend the lifestyle to others.

As commuter marriage becomes more widely accepted, there will be fewer raised eyebrows from significant others. Contacts with family members will become less awkward, but it will still be important for the partners to make sure children and parents understand the situation. A support system for long-distance marriage would also involve companies, who most surely will be employing individuals who have spouses in different locations. Primarily, employers could examine their policies in the light of the changing composition of the work force. With greater understanding of the benefits and problems of living together, apart, couples need not encounter demeaning questions such as, "How could you let her do it!"

Chapter Five

"Till Death . . .
or Career Relocation . . .
Do Us Part"

Corporate Commitments

"When I married 26 years ago, the career climate was different. My husband's career clearly has always come first, but he was very supportive of my working part time. Back in those days, though, a woman was made to feel guilty for pursuing a career. People would say, 'Don't you feel terrible about leaving your children?' I could never understand how playing bridge all day or going to charity teas was acceptable absence, but working was not. The women's movement was my great vindication. It finally said that working was all right. It was okay to do the things I wanted. If I could start out again today, I'd be more career-oriented and not so job-oriented. I had to leave a lot of good jobs when my husband's career required us to move. The truth is, I never thought about it. I always figured I'd find something in the new city, and I just went." Not so very long ago people were shocked when they heard of a wife refusing to relocate when a husband's corporation required it; today there may still be a few raised eyebrows, but people are no longer scandalized.

Couples are now faced with difficult relocation decisions, especially if they have children, but more and more of them tend to respond like Harriet and Yves Michel in an article in *Women's Work* (Reichers 1978:10). "Of course I've questioned if I am placing my own needs and career ambitions before the needs of my marriage and my family," said Harriet when she talked about her chance to become director of youth programs with the U.S. Department of Labor, a job that required her to move from their home in New York City to Washington, D.C. "But, in the end, I believe it will have been a good move for all of us." And it seems to have been a good choice for this couple. She was able to pursue a major career opportunity, and since Yves and their two school-age children remained in New York, he had the chance to become closer to them and to feel more capable of taking care of them. They did not have to experience the negative feelings of Larry and Brenda. Brenda gave up her job and followed Larry to San Francisco. She says, "I feel resentment against a system where making a career choice means ruling out a relationship. I'm not angry with him, he's as trapped as I am."

What is the history behind these either/or decisions, the career/relationship choice that couples have had to make until very recently? Were things always like this? Not at all. In preindustrial society, the family was the unit of both production and consumption. Family life and working life were one and the same. Work as a separate obligation did not exist, even though agricultural people had highly differentiated work roles that reflected family roles. Work was one of the general family obligations. In early industrial society, role segregation survived on the domestic scene in housework activities carried on there, but major income-earning activities became physically separated from family life. Work was something carried on by men outside the home. Domestic tasks, since they were not income producing, were not considered work nor an occupation.

As industrialization progressed two domains emerged, work and the family. People assume that the family regulates their lives; but when you explore your own personal experiences, it is obvious that our social units and lifestyle are organized around one thing—work. The time we have for the family, for leisure, for school, and even for sex is the period of time that is left over from work.

Our nation is based upon work, the work ethic; "idle hands the devil's work do," is what Granny used to say. It is a terrible dilemma for couples with children and a "Catch 22" situation for women. The family is at fault. Children are said to lack the "proper" attention at home because Mommie has listened to the siren song of business. Meanwhile, greedy organizations surprisingly, after all these years of telling you to stay home and take care of hubby and the kiddies, now lovingly encourage you to become part of the corporate community. Harvard even gave women the okay to enter their prestigious Master of Business Administration program in 1963. There were 2.6 *million* women in management and administrative positions by 1979. By 1984 the number of women in management had risen to 32 percent, up from 18 percent in 1972. There has been a quiet revolution, and whether the rewards of a career are "worth it" is no longer a question. Women in government, business, industry, and the professions are a fact. Work is the dominant influence.

"I was fired from my first job as a professor because I was pregnant. But I changed fields and got another job, something I'm glad about now. I had Mark on Monday and on Tuesday I called my boss and told him I'd be in on Thursday. I wasn't going to let my kids interfere with my career," says Madelyn, an attractive 45-year-old Gloria Steinem look-alike. Much more than is openly admitted, love and careers are irretrievably intertwined. The way people feel about each other is not based on some mystical chemical reaction totally separate from what each person is in the real world. Today, many couples stress that a partner's job and how well it is done and rewarded are the major bases of an attraction. "What I respect and love about my husband is his talent and ambition," says a commuter-marriage wife. If advancing your own career means stifling your partner's, it can unsettle the chemistry between you.

The Wall Street Journal (Getschow 1980:1) relates a typical story of a working-couple marriage. Laura was a 31-year-old vice president of personnel at Sanger Harris, a unit of Federated Department Stores Inc. She started as an assistant manager of executive development at a May Company Department Store in St. Louis. From the beginning her goal was to go as far as she could in management. As a result, her husband, Jim, an assistant manager at the same store, wasn't surprised when she accepted a job as corporate director of training and development at Federated Stores in Cincinnati, even though it meant a long-distance commute. "Laura felt that she was going to be doing a lot of traveling anyway and that the separation might even be valuable," said Jim. Laura agreed: "I thought I could devote my full attention to my new job during the week and to my husband on the weekends." But trying to make up for the lost time on the weekends was difficult. "I was extremely tired from putting in long hours at work. . . . Also, I was taking my job pressures home with me, and the strain was rubbing off on our relationship." After six months of commuting, Jim decided to take a "lateral transfer" to Cincinnati. Meanwhile, Laura's career was advancing rapidly, and before long she was transferred once again to Sanger Harris in Dallas. Jim reluctantly agreed to join her, but by this time, Laura was "two career levels above him"— a situation that was beginning to hurt their marriage. Jim later returned to St. Louis where it all began, and the couple was finally divorced.

Not all stories end this way, though. *Savvy*, a magazine for executive women, noted that their 1983 roster of outstanding women executives, "Twenty at the Top," included three women who successfully maintain long-distance marriages. Among them is Betty Sue Peabody, President and Chief Executive Officer of Citicorp Savings in Oakland, California. She was appointed to her position in 1982 and oversees $2.9 billion in assets, 80 branches, and 900 employees. Her commuter marriage is a long-distance one between Morris Plains, New Jersey, and Orinda, California. Another top female executive commuter is Joan D. Manley, Group Vice President—Books, Time Inc., New York, and Chairman of the Board, Time-Life Books, Alexandria, Virginia. She worked her way from secretary to chairman of the board in nineteen years of "hard work and good luck." Her commute is between her offices in Virginia and New York and a family home in Vermont. Shirley Young, born in Shanghai, China, with a B.A. from Wellesley College, is Executive Vice President of Grey Advertising Inc., New York. She is considered an expert on creativity—by which she means ideas, innovative thoughts, fresh approaches and insights. She believes, "What worked yesterday isn't the only way to do things." Her commuter marriage is between Detroit and New York. Getting to the top doesn't mean your relationship will fail even when you're a two-location couple. But it does seem certain that the higher up the career ladder you climb, the more likely you are to find yourself in a commuting situation.

One way to the top is through transfers within a corporation. For executives who take advantage of these moves, there is the possibility of becoming exceptionally knowledgeable about the company and the industry. Not only that; relocation increases an executive's visibility. Once a certain level is reached, whether you're a man or a woman, it's pretty much move or perish. Headlines state:

> "U.S. corporations are opening their managerial
> ranks to women as never before";
> "Women managers say job transfers present a
> growing dilemma";
> "Corporate women now eager to accept transfers";
> "Will husbands play second fiddle to exec wife?";
> "Some U.S. jobs turn strong marriages into weekend
> ones."

But how are corporations actually responding to commuter marriage? What are the problems of commuter marriage from the corporate standpoint? One of the most bizarre stories is told in *Working Women*. It is of interest because it contains many of the enigmas encountered in relocation of two-career couples.

A Manhattan man in his mid-30s recently landed a major marketing position with a firm in North Carolina. Gene Judd, president of the Judd-Falk executive-search firm in New York, made the match. The salary increase, says Judd, was about $10,000, and there were nice fringe benefits. But the man's wife, also in her mid-30s, had a flouishing career in data processing in New York. Like her husband, she was on the fast track. As a condition of the relocation, the husband made the new company pledge to help his wife find equal or better employment in her field in North Carolina.

Several weeks later, when the couple arrived at the new locale on the house-hunting and familiarization trip, the man's bosses-to-be were so taken by the woman's data-processing knowledge that they offered her a job, too.

There was a hitch, though: The company's employment policy prohibited hiring more than one member of the same family. Since the firm's data-processing needs were greater at the time than its marketing needs, the wife's job offer stood. She decided to accept it, but only if the firm helped find her husband equal or better employment.

In this case, relocation had a positive effect on the wife's career, and the husband was placed with a noncompeting firm in a job that offered the upward mobility he was seeking. (Hunter 1982:16)

Career Relocation and Spouses' Careers

The true story above is a rather extreme example, but it points up a new and very real dimension of career relocation that was never a problem back in the days when women stayed home—the effect of the relocation on a spouse's career. A husband can no longer assume his wife will pick up and move, taking whatever position she can get in the new location. A wife can't make this assumption either, but for women this belief probably never existed in the first place. Early socialization would tell her that he would probably not follow her. The career wife more likely had assumed that moving up would not necessarily require moving around. She may have believed that if they both had good, firm jobs in one location, things would stay that way. But instead, women's careers have attained the financial and personal importance that allows them to opt for new lifestyles. Commuting is one of these; rejecting one partner's advancement is another.

Phil and Lynn opted for commuting. They felt the economic factors couldn't be ignored, and there was also the idea of compelling personal fulfillment. Lynn is a 32-year-old marketing research executive who works for a major national consumer-goods company in New York. She supported Phil for seven years while he studied for his Ph.D. in political science. "When Phil got his degree last spring, he was offered a one-year post in Washington, D.C., but I was not at all prepared to make the move," said Lynn. "Phil had to acknowledge that I make three times the money he does. My future in the company looks great, and the skills I have are not easily transferable—especially in Washington, D.C.," said Lynn. "Then, I considered, what if Phil does get a university teaching job? I'll still always have the potential of making more money than he does. My career has to come first. We decided to have a two-city marriage—at least for now."

Roberta and Don opted for rejecting her possible advancement. "Sure I felt resentment, but marriage is working together. It's my stability. After we talked it out—he never thought of just saying yes and then simply dragging me along—I realized that at that given moment the higher income and Don's getting out of a dead-end job were more important than my job," said Roberta. "I really had a fit when I first heard about Don's promotion. I knew that my career would have to take a back seat for a while because with my experience and my wages I'd have trouble getting work just any place. I've found work here, but it's not as rewarding." Don says, "I don't know what we'll do next time; I can't say. What I do know is that we've certainly established a good pattern for making meaningful joint decisions."

Although corporate transfer as a route to advancement is showing signs of declining, it is still a fact that for the high-flyers in national companies relocation is a clear road to the top. But until recently many companies were reluctant to even suggest a transfer to a married woman for fear of promoting a domestic crisis. Some women as recently as 1978 were complaining that they never got the chance to try to work out the intricacies of a transfer because their companies simply refused to transfer them, assuming that it would disrupt their families. Psychologists believe that male corporate managers subconsciously suppress the notion of relocating married women because they internalize and personalize their decisions by imagining how they would feel if their own wives were asked to move. It is a covert mental process reflecting a paternalistic attitude. One person who was originally opposed to commuter marriage is Howard B. Johnson of the Howard Johnson restaurant chain. Doris Etelson, the first female vice president in the organization, reports, "He was concerned that it would either jeopardize my marriage or disrupt my business efficiency. He was wrong on both counts." Doris Etelson had been married for 32 years and commuting for 5. When she was offered the position in Boston, her husband Robert responded enthusiastically. "She supported me for years, and now she is entitled to whatever success she can get" (Gallese 1978:1).

Women are becoming eager to accept transfers as a route up the career ladder. Most of *Savvy's* "Twenty at the Top" advocate getting out if the job gets stale. In 1983 women accounted for about 6 percent of all corporate transfers, up from 3 percent in 1978 according to a survey of 607 corporations done by Merrill Lynch Relocation Management Inc. It is expected that the rate will soon grow dramatically. The unexpected thing is that the increase is coming at a time when corporations are cutting back on relocation. Transfers dropped 25 percent in the two years from 1980 to 1982. The retrenchment is due largely to the sharp rise in transfer costs, which doubled in that period. The proportion of managers willing to move more than once eroded from 84.4 percent to 76.3 percent between 1977 and 1981 according to a survey by Employee Transfer Corporation of Chicago, a relocation specialist. But relocation of women is running against this trend because the ranks of women executives are growing faster than company cutbacks in transfers. "If you choose not to go, chances are the company will be understanding—but, don't be surprised when you hear that the executive who *did* go gets the big promotion and you find yourself side-lined" (O'Toole 1982:38).

Not long ago the consensus was that IBM was merely an acronym for "I've Been Moved." John Pope, a public relations officer with International Business Machines, admits, "That used to be true—maybe way back in the sixties—but now less than 5 percent are moved. Unloading a residence is expensive. When we opened our facility in Tucson in 1978 a lot of people were brought in. Now we hire locally. Moving has flattened out." Another IBM official, T. E. Groskopf, Jr., a director of personnel resources, reported to the *Miami Herald* (O'Brien 1979:1C): "Transferring a single woman is not different from transferring a single man, but when it's a married woman we want to relocate, we have to ask ourselves, where does the husband fit. IBM makes every effort to relocate a spouse who works for the company, but it's getting more complicated. We're brainstorming for solutions now." John Pope says, "We work on a case by case basis. There is no policy. What we try to do is to accommodate employees within the bounds of business needs."

At General Dynamics Corporation there is no set policy, but things are getting more complicated. "On transfers it's difficult to work out. A promotion for one means a downgrade for the other. It's not so bad in a large plant in an urban area. Sometimes a job can be found for the spouse with another company. But we have a little plant in Arkansas with only 1,000 people; it's in the middle of nowhere—there's nothing we can do. If possible we try to work out a package for the family. We had one woman that was promoted and moved, but there was nothing we could do for the husband."

Hidden and Open Corporate Contracts

Corporations have, until very recently, had some automatic assumptions about relocation. Corporations transfer about 500,000 U.S. employees annually. Although "open" work contracts generally say nothing about relocation, it is frequently a part of the "hidden" contract that men can be moved to benefit the organization and will, of course, gladly move for promotion or career advancement. Meanwhile, corporations automatically assume that wives will accept that role of "trailing spouse." Today corporations quickly point out that the trailing spouse could be either a husband or a wife, but the truth is that, male or female, a trailing spouse can no longer be taken for granted.

Although corporate personnel people are very much aware of the problem, the decision-makers are reluctant to do anything about it. They are either unaware of the urgency, or when it comes right down to it they have very old-fashioned ideas about women and the nuclear family. Many chief executive officers continue with the idea of the hidden work contract between a husband, a wife, and the employer—the two-person single-career notion. Informal institutional demands assume that wives will entertain the organization's customers or guests, appear at appropriate social functions, support local charities, help the wife of the chief executive officer when required, and so on. They think wives should stay home, be supportive, and arrange a well-ordered domestic scene where the male employee can find refreshment rather than another set of work demands. In the fifties, when women were being pushed out of the workplace after heavy participation during World War II, corporations were actually asking for interviews with wives before making commitments to managerial-level males. Paying a wife for the work she was expected to perform was never a consideration, but she had to meet approval; she had to be "suitable" in the sense of being able to maintain a lifestyle appropriate to her husband's rank and the image of the corporation.

This is carried to extremes in certain situations such as the diplomatic corps and the military, where hidden contracts become quite explicit. Foreign service officers' wives are obliged to attend orientation courses before overseas assignments:

In the late sixties I attended the four-week program for State Department wives while Gerald was getting ready to go to Colombia. It was actually quite interesting, but then a terrific job opened up for me in Washington, and I didn't want to turn it down. I'd already given up one good job in California. They weren't too happy with me at the Foreign Service Institute. I was supposed to be in Spanish classes eight hours a day, and instead I was directing a special program for learning disabilities in Virginia. Gerald didn't like it either. I guess it was a reflection on him that he couldn't "control" me better. When it was time to leave for South America, I had some serious doubts. I was just beginning to move up again in my career, and I wanted to stay. But the State Department had counted on two people—we were supposed to be a team and all that rot. I finally went, I couldn't let Gerald down like that, but I was never able to recover from the loss of four years down there. When I came back, I had to start all over. Recently I heard that things have now changed. The foreign service wives are refusing to leave their own careers in Washington. Some couples are trying commuter relationships. Frankly, I'm glad. I doubt if State likes the idea of getting only one person, but I guess I always resented not being paid for my contribution.

Another foreign service officer and his editor wife thought it over for two years before he took an assignment in the Middle

East and she remained in the States. They feel it was a drastic solution, but neither was willing to jeopardize a career. Now the wife says, "Living apart is good for a marriage. It allows you a little breathing space."

There is considerable speculation that the reason enlistment and reenlistment are down in some branches of the military is because of the transfer policy that makes it so difficult for wives to pursue careers. An army spokesman said to Barbara Delatiner (1981:87) for *Working Mother* magazine, "We have no hard statistics on it, but we do know that we have nonretention, especially of noncommissioned, midcareer officers either because working wives don't want to leave their jobs when transfers come through, or because they can't—they need the money. So the husbands retire early to keep the families together." An air force officer's wife who was interviewed admitted that she simply got fed up with going to teas and luncheons, doing charity work, taking care of the wing commander's wife, and being an officer in the Wives' Club.

All we ever did was talk about how to raise money to paint, furnish, and decorate the base nursery and day care center. After fifteen years of this, I had to finally ask myself why all those day care centers weren't in tip-top shape. Gosh knows, we'd certainly spent a lot of energy and time on them. It began to look like a fraud. If women and kids had any status at all, the nurseries would have had some official priority and some money to keep them in shape. They wouldn't have been left for volunteer busy-work. The fact was, nothing we were doing had an impact, but we were at home to be supportive and to do the tedious work of moving the household and kids when our husbands flew off to a new assignment.

The point of the stories is simply that first, two-career marriage is on a rapid increase; second, many institutions still cling to the fading notion of a hidden work contract whereby they assume they will receive the services of two people for the price of one; and third, the career commitment of women is increasing, with the result that the commuter marriage option begins to appear more attractive.

Now let's look at what help corporations give to two-career couples as part of their relocation policies. What do relocation companies do?

Relocation Services and Counseling

Nobody knows very much about relocating dual-career couples. As IBM indicated, it needs a lot of brainstorming. But according to conservative predictions made from Bureau of Labor Statistics figures, by the end of the decade working husbands and wives will constitute at least 80 percent of all marriages. Relocating two-career couples is so complicated and can cause so much bitterness between a wife and a husband that many corporations don't even want to hear about it. A few years ago when male executives began turning down transfers because of their wives' careers, corporations began to turn more and more to relocation services and counseling. "Corporations asked us if we could make the noise go away," says Home Buyers Assistance Corporation vice president for marketing, Lee G. Chirgwin. "Male executives account for 95 percent of the transfers we handle. A woman executive has a tough time when her husband is transferred. She has probably achieved her status by virtue of her longevity in a city or a company, and she can't take that ticket with her when she moves" (O'Toole 1982:39). But in 1984 only 22 percent of more than 600 large corporations surveyed by Merrill Lynch Relocation Management were doing anything about it. "It used to be a pleasure to call in an executive and tell him he was being sent to Chicago or San Francisco. Now I've learned to brace myself for a negative response or at least a lukewarm one. His wife probably has her own thriving business, or is the top real estate broker for Century 21, or is a manager at General Foods. Men just don't want to move as much anymore," says a top personnel executive with a multinational corporation.

The Employees Relocation Council, a nonprofit advisory group, says a half-million employees were relocated in 1983 and that companies spent from an average of $46,800 per couple. Imagine for a moment that you and your spouse are one of those couples. Let's say you are a systems programmer with something called MM&G Long Lines in Virginia. You've just received word that you are needed in Morristown, New Jersey, to do specialized research work. It is a transfer promotion and you're delighted. Your spouse has a private school teaching position at Brockden Academy in Virginia, where you are now living. The director of the school is about to retire, and your spouse is optimistic about receiving the position at the end of the year. What exactly can you expect from the relocation service? The assistance given by the corporation and the relocation service will first of all depend upon the level of your new post, your value to the company, and the corporation's financial well-being. Since the chief characteristic of the relocation package is flexibility, you must ask for the maximum. Even poor institutions like state university systems can come across if they want you badly. The most generous package corporations are willing to give you would have the following benefits.

Moving Expenses. The company will help find the mover and pay for the packing, the move itself, and the unpacking of household goods. You can also negotiate to have the company move any unusual possessions like boats, travel trailers, hot-air balloons, ultra-light aircraft and so on. The company will also pay for your family travel expenses to the new community, including meals and hotel en route. Upon your arrival the company will also pay for the temporary housing and meals until your family is settled.

Housing Help. You are going to be concerned with homes on both ends of the move. Frequently, or perhaps occasionally, depending on the company and the location, your employer may offer to buy your current house at a fair market price. This frees up your cash to buy another house at the new location. Through what is called "mortgage interest differential," the company can help bridge the gap between the low-cost mortgage you now have in Virginia and the more expensive loan you're going to have to get on your new home in New Jersey when you move. If you decide to rent, a similar "renter's differential" can help ease you into higher rents in Morristown. Corporations also allow you time off for house-hunting trips. During these trips the relocation counselor will get your family together and talk about the new area: about housing, leisure activities, schools, advantages and disadvantages. The counselor presents a half-day multimedia demonstration and then takes you out and shows you the area. Since the counselor can't actually show you any house, you'll be "kicked out" to a realtor for that portion of your trip.

Cost-of-Living Differential. If you move, living in New Jersey will probably cost more than living in Virginia. You can ask the company to add whatever it takes to make up this difference to keep you from falling behind. Most companies will also pay you a month's salary to cover incidental expenses—there will be more of these than at first you imagine.

Help for the Working Spouse. This is the frosting on the relocation cake that most interests you and can mean avoiding a brush with divorce if the trailing spouse has greater job options. It is the issue that is shaping up as the *major* one in relocation for all families. Assistance ranges from concerted efforts to find the spouse a job with another company to informal measures such as job counseling and résumé preparation. About one-third of the 22 percent of large companies doing anything at all about this major relocation issue say they will try to find the spouse a job within the company. These are companies that don't have nepotism rules, but discussion of this issue will come later.

Right now, you have to decide whether or not to accept that transfer and the promotion that may be detrimental to your spouse's career. You will find that in the long run your marriage will be strengthened, because you must communicate with each other. You've got to decide which career takes precedence, for how long, and when. First you discuss the transfer before making any commitment. You take a "balance sheet" approach. What would work out best for each of you and both of you? List the two cities and compare. Compromise.

Okay, so let's imagine you decide you'll try to go to New Jersey and remain together. But neither of you is willing to return to a traditional situation where one assumes household tasks while the other "works." Your next step, then, is to enter into what is called "spouse bargaining" with MM&G and the relocation counselor. You go to your employer with the problem and a clear set of acceptable solutions. Are there any positions within the MM&G Company in the New Jersey location for which the teaching/private-school-director spouse would be qualified? The teaching spouse may have more generalized skills, while yours are more specialized. Usually the nonspecialist can relocate more easily, but MM&G has no positions suitable for your spouse, or maybe they have nepotism rules. Nevertheless, the relocation counselor is encouraging. They'll help your partner find a position in the Morristown area. Your spouse will receive career counseling and help in preparing a résumé. This service is valued at over $3,000. The résumé will probably be an indepth one, perhaps a functional résumé, with the right things highlighted and the less important things left out. And then what? Well, with luck, there will be a position in the New Jersey area that is acceptable at a salary that is not going to make your spouse feel downgraded and victimized.

But what happens when it doesn't work so nicely? You can both cry on the relocation counselor's shoulder. They can probably find your spouse "something," and the relocation service, if it's a good one, will continue working on your long-range goals. You may have some shaky moments in your relationship.

The thing to keep in mind is that the relocation services are just that—they are there to relocate you—BOTH of you. It is their business, and they are good at it. They will *not* offer alternative suggestions. They are working for the corporation to ease your move, but it is to be a move in the most traditional sense, where one of you is a trailing spouse. You will not hear talk about a halfway-point city where you both might live. You will not hear the relocation counselors suggest that you try out a commuter marriage. If you suggest such alternatives, you will be discouraged and hear horror stories of separation, divorce, and extramarital affairs. Corporations, at least a few of them, are mildly aware of the difficulties faced by two-career families, and relocation services, although designed mainly for more traditional arrangements, are responding with some help in "spouse bargaining." But what if you and your spouse weigh the issues, make out the balance sheet, and decide that what is best for both of you at the moment is to arrange a commuter marriage? How have corporations responded to this new social structure that clearly breaks the hidden work contract? Are there any services given by companies that would make commuting a more viable lifestyle?

Corporate Response to Commuter Marriages

Russ, a 38-year-old vice president of marketing with a major airline company, is the father of two children. He joined the airline in Dallas eight years ago and was soon promoted to an assignment in Phoenix. But his wife, June, wanted to stay in Dallas, where she worked in data processing, and she also wanted the children to complete a school year before moving. After a year of commuting Russ says, "the fabric of my family's life got ripped apart. Whenever I went home it was like a two-day honeymoon, Christmas, and New Year's Eve all packed into one. There was so much excitement it was unrealistic, but I began to feel more like a visitor than like a father and husband. Important things like discipline problems with my kids got put off."

American Airlines believes that stories like this one indicate hazards in commuting; so they have tried to discourage long-distance marriage. When American moved its corporate headquarters, the company adopted a policy requiring employees to make their principal place of residence where they work. The airline was afraid that many employees might leave their families behind in New York and commute to Dallas because they can fly free (Getschow 1980:1). Few companies have gone so far as American Airlines and actually refused to allow long-distance commuting. But there are in most institutions unwritten rules about career advancement and absence of the second person. Most companies take the attitude that if a person accepts a promotion, he or she should be willing to pay the price. If that means relocation, or long-distance commuting, they figure "that's their problem, not ours"; but the hidden contract says that you'll move up faster if you have a supportive spouse at your side to run a well-ordered domestic scene where you can find refreshment from work demands. Someone at your side who will provide work-related services: the hostess-with-the-mostest or the host with the greatest margaritas.

Although the two-person, single-career assumption is part of the hidden *work* contract, any deviation from this pattern is not considered to involve work but becomes a *domestic problem*, "their problem, not ours." Experts in organizational behavior are not so sure that the married single is strictly a domestic problem. It is work related, and it affects work performance. They note that without a support system there is a deep sense of isolation and detachment. Employees try to fill the void with excessively long hours on the job, and can turn to alcohol or other outlets. A few companies are listening to such statements and are taking some minimal steps to ease commuting difficulties for their employees.

Case-by-Case Consideration. Case-by-case consideration, although a very minimal response because there is no set policy, at least suggests that an organization is aware of the problems of two-paycheck families and of commuter couples. Perhaps they'd like the whole situation to go away and they're not facing it head-on, but they're giving it a side glance. It has at least entered the peripheral visual field.

Aluminum Company of America has been addressing career-couple problems on an informal case-by-case basis. The company has formed a task force to find out how companies can work together to facilitate spouse employment, but they have not considered how to facilitate commuter marriage. IBM Public Relations Office also says that cases are considered as they come up, in an impromptu fashion. The major position of this corporate leader is one of trying to decrease the overall number of transfers for all employees. "It simply is not cost-effective to move people around anymore."

General Dynamics also considers dual-career problems on a case-by-case basis. Personnel officials say that it is tough. "Recently we wanted to transfer one of our executives, but his wife has a very good business here in Mary Kay cosmetics. It wasn't that easy for her to pick up and move because her business was based on local knowledge of the area and her contacts. She was locked in. The couples found themselves in the position of one spouse blocking the other from corporate or business mobility. One spouse's career can limit the other's, and they get into this situation without any consciousness of it." Recent personnel journals are talking about "careers without conflicts," but this is difficult to achieve if we retain traditional notions of marriage (Flynn and Litzsinger 1981). The suggestion is that compatible careers can be achieved by planning; but few of us decide on our mates early enough to plan careers together. It is impossible to predict the future, and what is mobility today may be unemployment tomorrow. At General Dynamics a personnel specialist advises avoiding career selections based upon projections. "If you want to be a violinist, be a violinist." The idea here is to be a damned good violinist and you'll always have opportunities. But, "We wouldn't encourage long-distance commuting because it would probably be disruptive to the marriage unless you were very wealthy. A short term might be fine, maybe six months," says an executive of one large multinational corporation.

Use of Company Telephone Services. Telephone services are one of the most important supportive devices for commuter couples. While phone bills can be high in a commuter relationship, frequently over $200 per month, the use of leased company phone lines might cost only a fraction of that. "My wife wants to *talk*; fortunately the company pays the phone bill," said one employee of AT&T. International Business Machines report they will allow employees to use the internal telephone communication systems to a "reasonable and fair" amount, but since the system is internal, it is of no help unless both husband and wife are IBM employees.

"As much as we vowed not to call so often . . . there it was, every month Ma Bell with her horrendous monthly bills that tried to strangle our vital lifeline. I felt it was almost imperative to have daily contact because it helped to maintain a day-to-day closeness," said one commuter with a seven-year marriage and two years of commuting. Her husband reported, "We were used to coming home in the evening and having an exchange of what had happened to each of us that day. Some days there were triumphs and some days there were frustrations, but we always talked about it while we got ready to go out and jog together. I miss that more than anything when we're apart . . . that brief exchange of small daily happenings."

"We talk on the phone twice a day, and it's important for me in the morning because I need the send-off. When we're together I get a hug and a kiss and I go to work smiling and whistling. Now the phone call has to take the place of that," says a two-city-marriage husband. For high-income families, talking on the telephone helps avoid the sense of isolation. But few organizations supply help with phone lines or phone bills for middle-income couples as yet. More commuting couples should ask for this small perquisite that can be a top priority in maintaining employee morale.

Flexible Hours. Many commuter couples are university professors. One reason is the current job market, which makes obtaining even one university position difficult and two positions in the same place almost impossible. You can only "spouse bargain" when the market is right. Otherwise the risk is enormous, and you could lose two jobs, not just one. But the major reason academic people have so much success with commuter marriage is that they have very flexible schedules. The time that they *must* be available in classes or in their offices can frequently be squeezed into three or possibly even two days a week. This will mean that they'll work late into the night or be up at 4 A.M., but it also means that they can leave on Thursday night and return on Monday. For university faculty there are also the holiday breaks and a long summer vacation when couples can select where they'll spend the time together. Writing or research can be done with a great deal of flexibility. The actual hours spent working may be longer but far more flexible.

Another successful group of commuter couples are those where one partner owns a business—small or large. The truth is that ownership of a business may require far more than the 40-hour week, but a business owner may have the option of when to put in those hours. A commuter husband stated, "We married late in life and we both had our occupations firmly fixed. When I had to move to Colorado, Edith stayed in Alabama. She couldn't move her business, but it was well established and she could arrange a more flexible schedule to fly here to Denver, where I direct a computer center. It works out fine for us. It's like a holiday when we're together."

Most companies require a five-day week and 9 to 5 hours, making commuting very difficult, but some are experimenting with flexible hours. The estimate is that about 6 percent of

American employees work for companies that give them some control over their working hours. One flexible time option sets a core period during the middle of the day when everyone must be present. An employee then has the option of arriving or leaving within a wider range of hours so long as the minimum amount of time is arranged. This system would allow a commuter spouse to arrive late on Monday and leave early on Friday. Another option used by American Airlines' ticket-tabulation center allows workers to change hours from day to day. Others, such as Northwestern Mutual Life Insurance Co. in Milwaukee, ask employees to set a fixed daily schedule.

Even the federal government has experimented with making the 40-hour week flexible. Civil service employees can "bank" hours by working overtime and "borrow" them back later. Before this could be done, though, Congress had to suspend the overtime prohibition for civil service employees. This system would allow commuters to work longer hours one week in order to take extra time off for travel or time with family the following week. A problem for private employers using flexible time is that they would have to be free to vary hours without paying overtime. Flexitime schedules can be requested from employers, and would be of great help to commuter couples dealing with both an important job and an important relationship.

Reimbursement for Weekly Airfare or Auto Expense. Pepper and Nelson met in a very romantic setting. Pepper was in Ecuador teaching English at the university, and Nelson was a University of New Mexico graduate student winding up a six-month research project there. They have been commuting ever since. Pepper now teaches English as second language at Pima Community College in Tucson while Nelson is in San Diego teaching anthropology. They feel they are lucky to have spent only $5,647 on airfare. Do any organizations help commuter couples with the expense of travel between their two residences? Possibly, but survey information, interviews, and reviews of all the articles written on the subject have mentioned only one. It is the case of Karen and Jack Pfeffer in *Executive Female* magazine. Xerox is paying airfare for Jack's Texas–California commute.

Karen manages professional placement and development for the Atlantic Richfield Company in Los Angeles. Jack directs long-range planning for office of the future products for Xerox in Dallas. So every Friday night, Jack Pfeffer heads for the Dallas/Ft. Worth airport and flies to Los Angeles where he spends the weekend.

"It's been very rough," Karen readily concedes, "especially on Jack. The weekly commuting, on top of his already hectic schedule, is exhausting. And the separation is difficult for both of us. We call each other several times a day."

Besides the physical and emotional toll, the arrangement brings the added financial cost of maintaining two homes—a house in the California suburbs and a condominium in Dallas—enormous telephone bills, and some commuting expenses, although Jack's company reimburses them for the weekly airfare [emphasis is mine]. (Hogan 1980:34)

Yet, Karen believes the decision to stay behind in Los Angeles when Jack transferred to Dallas ten months ago was the right one. Absorbing commuting costs is still a rare position for a company, but it's not an impossible one. As couples reach higher-income executive levels in organizations and as more and more two-career couples become permanent fixtures in the work force, "spouse bargaining" will be broadened to include this option.

Nepotism Rules. Nepotism restrictions were designed to prevent favoritism in hiring positions. The term was first used in medieval times and referred to favoritism shown to "nephews" by high-ranking ecclesiastics, such as bishops who had authority over church districts. The situation changed, of course, but nepotism rules became not merely stumbling blocks for women who sought careers, but immovable barriers. The new benefits designed to address the two-paycheck family include the relaxation of nepotism rules. Firms are gradually easing restrictions against family members working for the same company.

Ellen says nepotism restrictions have controlled her entire life. "Tom and I had identical backgrounds. We both had our doctoral degrees in history from major universities. We were married right after we graduated in 1963. Tom immediately got a position at a large university in Texas, and I followed thinking that I would be able to convince them of how great I was—I had more publications than Tom, a better grade point—and that they'd hire me too. They never really did. I sat around the whole first year trying to do some research and helping Tom. The university had nepotism rules. We both talked with the president, but it didn't change things. He felt it was risky to have two people from the same family working for the same institution. It had nothing to do with my qualifications or experience." Ellen continued, "The president was very traditional and told us, 'Employees tend to become disgruntled; if you have one person coming home discontented, it affects the other person; so then there are two of you unhappy.' I thought the idea was ridiculous, but the attitude is one that is not uncommon because it assumes the Victorian stance that a wife is 'part of' her husband. She can have no ideas nor identity different from her spouse. It also presupposes that a wife should be there . . . be supportive, be soothing . . . when the out-of-humor husband returns from the cold cruel world."

"We struggled with the situation for almost two years," said Ellen. "I was having a difficult time. Finally the university agreed to let me teach part time. It meant that I would get none of the benefits of a full-time professor: no possibility for promotion, no tenure, no insurance, no health care, and very little salary. As pitiful as the offer was, I snapped it up. At least I'd be working, and I had some sort of professional affiliation to give my research credibility."

"I did it for thirteen years. Part time, picking up scraps. Meanwhile, Tom became department chair. I was not given a full-time position until I brought legal action against the university. The nepotism rules were not done away with; they were only loosened so that academic couples could both be employed full time. There was the hitch, however; if a husband or wife was in an administrative/supervisory position, the spouse could not work in that department. The rationale this time was that evaluation of performance would not be impartial—is it ever? But this meant that I could not work in history. They finally put me into political science and that's where I am today," says Ellen, "Still an assistant professor."

With the relaxing of nepotism rules, it becomes easier for couples to find positions in the same location, but this isn't always the ideal situation either. Before discarding the idea of commuter marriage in favor of working together, it is best to be aware of the pitfalls. When you both work in one place, the identity of one of you is apt to be lost. It is usually the woman's. One woman interviewed related this incident: "We were in an area meeting. My husband expressed an opinion. The chair turned to me and said, 'Of course, you agree, don't you, Rosemary?' I turned and said, 'No!' He seemed surprised and even a little shocked—after sputtering a bit he said, 'Well, ah, doesn't this cause problems for you at home?' "

A professional partnership can be rewarding, but when you work closely together each day a method must be developed for softening the cut-throat critical and competitive nature of some work, or it can erode the husband-wife relationship. Criticism is necessary to maintain standards and stimulate creativity, but you have to learn how to criticize with love. It's easier said than done, though. Some couples suggest that you must accept criticism in work as different from attacks on a person.

Another reported, "I think it might be a problem to work in the same department or the same company if you were in competition. But for Ralph and me, it has been ideal. We met at work, we share the same interests, it's our bond. It's easier for us, though, because we're not on the same level; Ralph is an associate professor, and I'm an instructor. As an instructor I don't have to compete. I'm on a yearly renewal contract; so I don't have to do research or worry about tenure. I don't know what will happen in the future. Sometimes it bothers me that in the classroom I'm doing exactly the same thing as those full professors, but I'm not making even half the money."

When asked about whether disillusionment over work situations was contagious when working in the same organization, Ralph's wife, Christina, replied, "If one of us comes home at night upset about something that happened on the job, the other doesn't reinforce that annoyance. What we usually do is more objective and not simply supportive. One of us says something like, 'Well, maybe you should look at it this way.' Getting a different perspective really helps."

One couple interviewed had shared a job for four years. They had literally done *everything* together: team teaching, encouraging each other's research, being mentors to students, attending conferences, caring for three children. "Eventually the advantages became disadvantages. We needed private career interests. We had slowly become cut off from the rest of the world. It became a kind of incestuous approach that was nonproductive. We needed to develop individual identities, but it was hard to get out because by now we'd both been working only part time, or at least that's the way hiring committees looked at us. It took awhile, but we agreed that the first one to get an offer would leave the other. When the offer came, I was terrified, but things stabilized and now I enjoy my freedom. Our long-distance relationship has been successful for a year and a half now."

Conflicts of Interest. If the nepotism rules don't get you, the "conflict of interest" problems may. When a husband and wife work for competing companies, for example, they can wander into conflict-of-interest situations by talking about the wrong subject over dinner. Since it may be illegal to discriminate against applicants on the basis of the spouse's occupation, personnel managers are careful how they interview prospective employees. For instance, they may ask, "Are you familiar with the copper industry?" hoping to trap the applicant into saying "My husband has worked in it for ten years." Some couples try to solve the problem by not talking shop at home. They have a "gentleperson's agreement" to hold out trade secrets or to put them through a "mental shredder" on the way home. A representative for the John Wiley and Sons publishing house said, "We have so many executives in this business who are married to each other that we have stopped worrying about conflicts of interest." But other fields are less tolerant, especially where millions of dollars can be involved in patent rights. Dr. Melvin McKnight, an Arizona specialist in organizational behavior, said, "Above all, chief executive officers of corporations have to consider what is best for the company. That takes precedence over any personal or individual considerations." So spouse bargaining in relocation is more difficult because the position for the trailing spouse must be found with a noncompeting company. Commuting then becomes an attractive alternative to relocation, if concessions such as flexible hours, telephone lines, and possibly a commuting allowance can be bargained for.

Job Sharing. Two people, one job, is an alternative that has been restricted mainly to academic couples here in the United States. Academic couples frequently ask to share positions because of job shortages, and shared appointments are welcomed at small, liberal arts colleges because they can widen the range of faculty talent without adding the cost of additional jobs. It is a nice arrangement for solving child care problems for young families, but the drawbacks can be considerable. There can be too little outside stimulation. There can be too much marriage. Although there's more to talk about, there may be less to listen to—but more to fight about. Couples report that shared jobs can test the weak areas of any relationship, perhaps more so than commuting.

But the primary tension lines for job-sharing couples come from external influences of a plainly sexist ideology. Because they are married, there is the assumption that couples will agree on most issues. What if they don't; can they have two votes? Probably not. Whose opinion is most valued? A job-sharing clergy couple reported that more people rely on the male as the "real" professional. A job-sharing university faculty couple report the same thing.

A second tension line develops from the part-time stigma. Traditionally part-time employment has low status and connotes a temporary arrangement. These perceptions impact upon the job-sharing individuals and stigmatize them as having little commitment, low motivation, and minimal qualifications. There is an aura of distrust even among colleagues who have reviewed and approved their qualifications. People can't readily accept the desire to spend more time with family and in leisure activities as legitimate because work is what organizes lifestyles and has high value. Job sharing seems "unprofessional."

Economic exploitation is a third stress point for job sharing couples. What frequently happens with a culture oriented toward the work ethic is that each spouse devotes more than half time to the job—not so much from employer demands as from ambiguous boundaries and from an attempt to do more than an average job to prove the benefits of job sharing to the employer. Some couples prefer, if possible, to share one and a half jobs. They feel this more nearly approximates a fair value for the ratio of work produced to wages paid. But job sharing, because of the part-time status of each earner, is usually less well paid in actual dollars, and the added health insurance, dental insurance, retirement, and other peripheral benefits are frequently missing. Nevertheless, there is a small but growing trend toward job sharing; but if you consider this alternative, arrangements must be initiated by you.

Child Care. The 5.5 million working mothers of preschool children are perhaps the fastest-growing segment of the female work force. Conservative estimates say that at least 43 percent of married mothers with children under 6 now work. This is true for commuter couples as well as for two-paycheck households that are more traditional and live in one location. But another important fact is that there are simply fewer children. People are less children-oriented and more self- or career-oriented. Having children is no longer a social obligation; it is merely one available option that can be freely chosen or rejected.

Caroline Bird in *The Two-Paycheck Marriage* (1979:158) notes that "historically women have always been able to avoid pregnancy when there was high motivation to do so." During the depression of the thirties they did it without the benefits of modern contraceptive methods. During the late sixties and seventies, when they were looking forward to something exciting, such as political action or new careers, they always remembered to take along their pills. Women have children when there is nothing more exciting to do—when they were forced out of war jobs after World War II, when they are locked into welfare in big city ghettos, when they are locked into cottages in suburbia. One woman related, "When I was married in 1950, I was fired from my job as a stewardess with United Air Lines. We didn't want to have children right away—it seemed best to have a stable marriage first. I started doing charity work, went to a lot of teas, played bridge three afternoons a week, joined the ex-airline stewardess group 'Wilted-Wings.' In less than a year I thought I'd go crazy. I was used to traveling all over the country meeting strange and interesting people. My husband didn't want me to work. One day I confided my distress to a close friend. 'Why don't you have a baby?' said she. She had just had three girls in rapid succession, and she had plenty to do. It seemed like a good idea, an escape. Now, if I am honest, and someone were to ask me 'Why did you want a baby?' I would have to admit that it was to cure my boredom. I don't think it's a very good reason for having children."

Since there is now plenty to do, there will be fewer children for working couples, and working couples who have commuter marriages will have even fewer children. The baby panic may not arrive for couples in two-location marriages. There are just too many better things to do. They will not want to organize the family around children because they are too busy organizing their lives around their jobs and each other. The time, money, and travel obligations involved in commuter relationships make objective barriers to parenthood. But what are companies doing to help?

The answer must be indefinite. Some companies have introduced day care in recent years, thinking it makes economic sense. It reduces absenteeism, pacifies unions, and helps to retain experienced employees. The results have been mixed, because there is simply not much knowhow on successful company-sponsored day care as yet. Child care "specialists," mostly male pediatricians and child psychoanalysts, have been stressing the importance of "mothering," and they have meant *by mother*, on the emotional development of children. But research by Harvard University psychologist Jerome Kagan and a New York City study reveal that intelligence scores of infants raised in day care centers were significantly higher than those of children raised by parents or in neighbors' homes (Hogan 1980:36). Now more fathers are becoming deeply involved in parenting, and this shift may bring about more interest on the part of corporations to consider on-site day care facilities. AT&T reports that its day care facilities are underutilized at present because parents prefer to leave their children near home. But this situation may change as the number of women in the work force increases. General Dynamics is now considering opening on-site day care centers. Meanwhile, Polaroid Corporation and the Ford Foundation, rather than providing on-site facilities, have chosen to give partial reimbursement to employees for day care expenses. Executive couples say they prefer professional child care in the home, but the cost is high, a minimum of $175–$200 a week.

Scenarios for the Future

The commuter marriage survey contained the question, "Did your employer or your spouse's employer respond in any way to your decision to live separately? The overwhelming reply to this question was "no." Some commuters said, "My employers did not know," or "We did not make it known." Only one respondent said that her employer "facilitated finding a job for spouse." Two-city couples tend to talk very little about their commuting arrangement. Because of the unique, nontraditional nature of the relationship, that little is said about it is perhaps necessary at least for the moment. Talk to outsiders is limited to people who are not likely to be threatened by innovation or the unconventional. Employers, for instance, might fear that they would not have the full commitment from an employee whose domestic support system was 2,000 miles away; or the reliability of the employees might be questioned. The stability of the employee's marital relationship could be in doubt. Yet none of these things are at issue. The commuter merely has high commitment to both the job and the relationship. But in spite of the apparent secrecy when it comes to telling employers about a nontraditional marital arrangement, everyone is very much aware of the increasing occurrence of commuter marriage. The interesting thing is that almost any time you begin talking about commuter marriage to any one at all, there is a universal response, "Oh yeah, I know a couple who . . . ," or "A flight attendant based in Phoenix had a fire fighter husband who lived in Florida, and they . . ." Everyone knows at least one commuter couple, and "60 Minutes" has done a segment on the subject. Nevertheless, information seems to be exchanged principally on a grapevine basis, and couples frequently hesitate to mention it to employers.

But what gains will the increasing incidence of long-distance marriage bring to employees, employers, and the economy in general?

Gains to Employees. Self-fulfillment. Absolutely! There is no longer a need for career sacrifice. No one need be the victim. Neither partner must lose in order for the other to gain. "The opportunity to develop independently," says one commuter. "I think temporary separations are great," says another, "because they allow one to distinguish the problems that reside in the relationship versus the ones that are individual. Also, I love the independence." A third said, "It made my husband very proud when he discovered he had a wife very capable of taking care of things in his absence." "I have complete happiness and satisfaction in my personal life and business," says a female president of a New York management consulting firm. A male university professor who is a commuting spouse says, "I lost weight." Another spouse replies about his two-city marriage, "It was the chance to pick up on a once-in-a-lifetime opportunity that two-career couples can't pass up."

Gains to Employers. Career-motivated individuals—people that are willing to give work responsibilities and career advancement top priority. Many long-distance spouses frequently work 14- to 18-hour days. "There's a plus factor in weekend marriage. It allows me to work late and schedule appointments at all hours without worrying about what my husband had planned," says a woman in marketing. Employee turnover decreases because husbands and wives aren't always seeking positions outside their companies in order to relocate with a spouse as long as their commuter arrangement is receiving support. This support could be in terms of tangibles such as flexible work schedules and use of telephone lines, or intangibles such as trust and a feeling of group membership.

U.S. corporations are now experimenting with a new style of management called Theory Z. This mode of operation is being adapted to American organizations from a model that has allowed such great success and increased productivity in Japan. One of its chief components is specialization in an organization rather than in a particular job. Members of the organization develop a strong group identity that can be particularly valuable to a spouse who is in a commuter marriage. The organization itself becomes the family support system the commuter needs while away from the more traditional family situation, and a firm sense of company loyalty develops.

The compartmentalization of domestic and work environments that two-city marriage creates can also be a gain for an employer. What occurs is that when the employees are there, whether at home or at work, they're all there. "When I pull out of the driveway on Monday morning for my 250-mile drive to work, I leave the high-school cheerleader problems and domestic worries like the crumbling driveway," reports a director of employment at First Interstate Bank. "I enjoy the time by myself to totally concentrate on my work effort. Right now my position is very demanding. It requires a 100 percent effort, and I can give it that," says a television station production manager. But does this devotion to the workplace cause problems for the family? Not often in our work-oriented society. One husband told his wife, "You're more fun to be around now that you can talk about the good things in your job."

Gains for the Economy. How will people profit from commuter marriage? How may it affect the economy? There will be two salaries. This means that there will be two paychecks to spend, but commuter couples won't be spending those two paychecks in the traditional way, even though they are part of the acquisitive generation. Their lifestyle necessitates something quite different from the usual luxury items that the second paycheck generally brings.

First, they will spend money, lots and lots of money, on transportation. All types of transportation. Airline ticket sales are one aspect, but trains, buses, and private autos will also be used, depending on the distance and on the local situation. The wonderful bullet trains used in Japan and Europe would be ideal for commuting couples, but we have none of those at the moment. Maybe in the future. Right now for the commuter who is less than 500 miles away from a spouse, it is absolutely essential to have not one but at least two automobiles that are in excellent condition and new enough so they're ready to go each weekend. "I put 24,000 miles on my new Honda between mid-December and May," said Dick, "and my wife was doing half the driving. We didn't count how much we spent on gasoline, but I know it was over two tanks a week."

After the essential transportation expense, there is the extra housing. Commuter couples must have two homes, and even when one location is considered "home," the other residence can be equally large and elaborate. Some commuting couples maintain two condominiums. Some have a house and an apartment. Sometimes the second home is only a tiny 14-square-foot apartment. Commuter couples' homes are generally less a projection of their social status than a reflection of their interests and tastes as individuals. One couple reported having two condominiums, both of them right on a golf course, so that wherever they were they could indulge their love for golf. Regardless of the type of residence, there are always two. This means a duplication of all household effects: two sets of furniture; two sets of linens; pots, pans, cooking utensils for both homes; two sets of tableware and dishes; two pipe racks; two hammers; two vacuum cleaners; two cans of scouring powder; two crystal brandy goblets in each of two china cabinets. Some couples maintain two wardrobes so that there is no need for packing and unpacking on each visit. The duplication of households can bring considerable profit to merchants.

Restaurants also profit from busy two-residence families. One couple interviewed stated, "We enjoy dining out with friends at some pricey restaurants in San Antonio. It gives us a good feeling to know we can afford such luxuries." Part of the honeymoon atmosphere that is so evident when commuters talk about their time together comes from the specialness of the occasion, and a part of this specialness is getting away from the usual household task of cooking. But surprisingly these couples, when they do cook, seem to use fewer prepared, packaged food products. They like to "cook from scratch," and some make a hobby of it. In fact, cooking for some survives only as a hobby. It is sometimes a means of relaxation when they are alone or becomes a two-person cooperative project when they are together. One couple reported that in their "home" they have a his-and-hers kitchen—both husband and wife have range, oven, sink, and preparation areas. They cook together in this comfortable room as a recreational activity.

The commuter couple must spend money on transportation and two homes, but they also spend large amounts on time- and labor-saving devices. Time is the major concern for commuters. With high career commitment and high personal-relationship commitment, couples constitute a good market for anything that will cut down the time spent on routine household necessities. What kind of help is on the way for them in the way of time-saving innovations?

For years Ma Bell's contribution has been the yellow pages, "Let your fingers do the walking." But now more enterprising entrepreneurs are coming up with ingenious and comprehensive devices to help the commuter couple. The banks are now talking about "electronic funds transfers." These are machines that permit banking at all hours. An entire month's bills can be paid with a single phone call. The 800 numbers accommodate the need to take care of personal business at off hours. Telephone food delivery services are no longer limited to pizza. You can get a full selection of dishes from Hungarian goulash to Peking duck. Take-out gourmet services are springing up in major cities across the country. If something is needed suddenly, an impromptu dinner can be ordered early in the day and appear in the kitchen, sometimes in an attractive wicker hamper, before the guests arrive.

Catalog sales are booming, and the quality is way up too. You're no longer limited to *Sears* and *Penney's*. Now there are specialty catalogs selling everything from foods and fruit, like *Harry and David*, to elegant "dress for success" classic business suits for women, like *Saint Laurie Ltd*. You can buy your hunting and fishing equipment from *Cabela's*, your camping things from

REI, and your outdoor sports clothing from L. L. *Bean* in Maine. There must be dozens of mail-order toy catalogs, and dozens more from which you can choose your spring and summer garden. Some shopping by mail is going one step further; they now offer nationwide, personalized consulting and shopping services for the busy executive. Clients pay an annual membership fee, usually about $30, and complete a questionnaire about personal characteristics and lifestyle. A consultant then works with each customer, providing services ranging from advice on single purchases to proposing an entire wardrobe. Clients can purchase nothing, one or several outfits, or the entire wardrobe.

Probably the latest thing in shopping is video purchasing. Companies are now saying that within a very short time you will be able to turn on your personal computer and see a whole fashion show from which to select, or dial the housewares department and purchase the new linen for your Thanksgiving dinner table. The dinner, of course, will be delivered by the take-out gourmet service. Parisian Inc., a chain of Alabama department stores, has put its Christmas gift catalog on videodiscs. The computer poses questions about the recipient then displays pictures of three recommended gifts along with some stocking stuffers.

The search for qualified child care and household personnel can be agonizing and extremely time and energy consuming. One commuter wife said she had spent over a year looking for adequate child care and was still not totally satisfied. Now couples can turn increasingly to agencies which specialize in this field. For such agencies, there has been a very rapid upturn in business as more women enter and remain in the work force. The boom has caused many agencies to hire additional placement counselors specializing in domestic services and has encouraged other agencies to broaden their base by moving into the field. "The swelling of the ranks of executive and professional women has had a ripple effect on the employment of women in general by creating a substantial number of new jobs within the homes of America," said a West Coast placement specialist reporting to *Executive Female* magazine (Hogan 1980:37). *Merry Maids*, a national professional home cleaning company which offers a complete training and sales system, is offering franchise territories in the West for $11,500 including supplies and equipment. So if you're looking for a business opportunity, the best place may be in services for the growing number of two-paycheck households.

The massive influx of women into the working world has begun to reshape American business. It has been a positive influence on the economy, helping to maintain the $3.363 trillion gross national product in 1983. Estimates suggest that there are now over 26 million couples earning two salaries, and these couples have enlarged the nation's affluent class of families with annual income of $25,000 or more. Two paychecks have also been a cushion against recent economic downturns and unemployment. Dr. Peter Raynolds of the College of Business Administration, Northern Arizona University, states, "The number one shortage in American industry today is talent. Women are filling that shortage." But industry can help by moving away from action and thinking based on the traditional single-wage-earner family and acknowledging and facilitating new family patterns such as two-location marriage. Business organizations that do will find themselves ahead in the race to find and retain talented employees.

Chapter Six

"With All My Worldly Goods, I Thee Endow"

Two Paychecks and No Extra Pay

Extra money isn't extra anymore. Commuter couples were asked, "How is the extra money from your dual-career marriage spent?" The overwhelming response was, "What extra money?!" In fact, the wording of the question itself perpetuates the erroneous assumption that the norm is a single-paycheck household and that two paychecks must indeed be something extra—the cakewinner premise. The reality of the economic situation shows that the present norm is two paychecks, and the economic survival of a family demands two paychecks, but nevertheless the image of the one-paycheck family remains vivid. Two paychecks are a means of dealing with the high cost of living for young couples and a means of planning for future retirement for older commuter couples. One dual-residence husband stated, "We're in our mid-50s, both of us on our second marriage. Our children are now in their mid-to-late-20s and finally becoming self-supporting. We've been commuting for three years because when we married we could not find jobs in either of the cities where we were working. We've got to plan for retirement now by putting money aside in investments, but it's taking the two paychecks to do that. In our parents' time, they were able to do it easily on one salary. Now, without two, we can't do it at all."

The Wall Street Journal (Gottschalk 1983:1) quotes real-estate consultant Lewis Goodkin as saying, "This is the first generation that in all probability will never live in a home as large or as nice as their parents' house. The post–World War II 'baby boom' generation who are now 25-to-34-year-olds trying to buy their first homes find that they have to pay more of their incomes for smaller living space. They make do with tiny doll houses with Murphy beds, skylights, and wall mirrors and only manage to do this on two incomes."

So, the notion of an *extra* income must be rejected as a thing of the past, and this is doubly so for two-city couples, who report, "For us there isn't any extra money. We spend it mostly for traveling." Commuter couples seem to have a few investments, and perhaps a mutual savings account. They meet expenses and pay for travel, and the tiny doll houses available meet their housing needs better than the traditional large family residence in the suburbs.

Right now, wives contribute approximately 40 percent of the earnings of working couples, and the weekly earnings median of two-paycheck couples is 43 percent higher than the weekly earnings of families where only the husband works. Two paychecks seem to make recession-proof relationships. Nevertheless, culturally we seek to maintain the illusion that She is making pin money and He is the real support of the family. At least we have traditionally done so, and in the past the fantasy was maintained by an elaborate web of money management methods. These schemes for two-paycheck management are still around and must be explored before we go to the more complex situation that exists for dual-residence couples.

Men have become accustomed to the idea that they are doing a great thing when they bring home a paycheck. And indeed, according to the unwritten marriage contract, they are. Underlying the laws on age of marriage, whereby the male had to be older than the female to wed, was the notion that boys needed extra time to acquire career training and prepare to earn a living. A husband had the right to select where the couple should live because it was his work that determined the family domicile. A husband who brought home a regular paycheck was a "good provider" and worthy of respect and admiration. This idea is firmly with us today, although some may imagine that things have changed. The good provider notion is clear in the statement of Terry Bradshaw (Kaplan 1979), Pittsburgh Steeler quarterback and many-time Super Bowl star. Bradshaw talks about his long-distance marriage to JoJo Starbuck, the Olympic champion ice skater and star of the Ice Capades. "She can't throw football in my face because it's football that pays for those mink coats, the Mercedes-Benz, the trips around the world. All I ask is more of a return on my investment than I'm getting right now [with a commuter relationship]." A paycheck is a "gift of love"; yet there has to be some return on the "investment" in the form of domestic support. The Bradshaw-Starbuck marriage didn't make it.

JoJo Starbuck stated in the 1979 interview, "He'd say to me: 'If you really loved me, you wouldn't go away.' But it's not that I don't love him; it's just that I want other things, too. I never thought you had to give up all the other wonderful parts of your life in order to be married" (Kaplan 1979:40). Starbuck is simply stating the idea expressed by others who state "I am entitled to do work that I care about. Its value to me is at least as important as its value to the world."

There are, however, the two paychecks, and Caroline Bird believes that financial decisions of dual-earner couples are 98 percent emotion and 2 percent practicality. One young commuting wife almost screamed her response to the question about extra money: "It is MINE! It's not *extra* money." Traditionally, since women weren't supposed to have a paycheck in the first place, there is plenty of emotion involved in what to do with it. Critical sore spots can develop if a wife is promoted faster than a husband and her income becomes greater than his, and once again the law comes into the picture, making the husband head-of-household and thereby minimizing whatever a wife earns. Bird (1979:130–36) discusses four ways that dual-paycheck couples think about the threat of her money.

Pin money couples segregate her money from the "real support." It is to be spent on herself, or earmarked for something nice but unnecessary. This saves him the pain of dealing with it.

It's "Aw shucks, honey, it's yours to blow as you please." The notion that money belongs to men is there, however. He is merely being generous and "gives" her the right to keep her money (as long as it is spent for the "right" things). Among commuters, there are very few pin-money couples. The cost of two residences is too great, the spouses too independent, and their lives too compartmentalized.

Earmarker couples deal with the threat of her money by acknowledging that she can "help," but that it is actually his money that the family really lives on. He helps her with the dishes, and she helps him by paying for the new car or the piano. Frequently, though, the earmarker money slips into paying routine family bills. It is difficult to keep it separate, and the "cakewinner" rarely eats cake. It's the same old meat and potatoes, fishing tackle, and Ruger 44 Magnum.

Pooler couples put it all into one pot. It becomes "our money" to be budgeted together. The emphasis is on the family as one unit. "I'm not working for me," says the young wife, "I'm working for us." But as Bird notes, pooling doesn't mean joint decisions or equal say. Nevertheless, most single-residence couples choose this method. For commuters it is more difficult to pool because bank accounts are generally separate and often in separate cities. Pooling for commuters is more likely to be limited to long-term savings or investments.

Bargainer couples look the threat of her money full in the face and accept it at full value. They assume that a paycheck belongs to the person who earns it. They divide household expenses; they split every bill down the middle or in proportion to their incomes. Single-residence couples then put "their" money for household expenses into a box, a drawer, an old brown wallet or whatever. Out of this they pay housing, food, utilities, joint entertainment, and sometimes transportation. What each has left over goes for personal expenses, but disagreements can happen, especially if her leftover money buys expensive, visible items. There's also the problem of who really owns what.

Most commuters seem to use some variation of the bargainer method of money management. They definitely assume that a paycheck belongs to the one who earns it. The variations

they select depend on the two incomes. If there is great disparity between the incomes, such that a partner could not manage
without help, there is a greater tendency to become poolers.
But, since commuters live together, apart, household expenses
are divided down the residence rather than being divided down
the middle for routine items such as personal expenses, food,
and utilities. Spouses maintain themselves and their domiciles
while they are apart. When the couple is together there is sharing of expenses for joint entertainment, vacations, and family
obligations such as private schools, child care, and major
household items. Some couples, rather than sharing these expenses while together, alternate in paying them. This month she
pays; next month he pays.

Fewer women actually hide their paychecks now, but
many still see to it that the paycheck shrinks somewhere between the office and the front door like old-fashioned Levis in a
hot wash tub. This allows the husband to maintain what Bird
calls the "gold standard." "I bring home the gold, and I set the
standards." Commuter couples rarely know exactly where the
money goes or who is paying for what; so there is less of a strain
on the male ego to maintain the breadwinner image. One couple
became so confused they had to pay penalties on income tax
because each assumed that the other was filing, and before they
realized that no one was, it was too late.

Many commuter couples find themselves in the position
of spending all the money they make on the logistics of making
it. The financial situation of long-distance marriage is such a
complicated yet fascinating one that *Money* magazine has had
several articles on the topic. One article appeared in 1981 and
discussed the "fortnightly affair" marriage of two university professors, Carla and William Phillips. The Phillipses are college
history teachers who work 1,500 miles apart. She is in Minneapolis and he is in San Diego. When their story appeared, they
had been commuting for seven and a half years and were planning on continuing their commuting life even though it was
expensive because they had settled comfortably into their far-
flung jobs. During this time, Carla and William have seen each
other only on vacations, leaves of absence, and alternate week-

ends when either he flys to Minneapolis or she flys to San Diego. "The expense is horrible, moans Carla. But there's no end in sight" (Seixas 1981). The Phillipses are unswervingly committed to their teaching careers.

What are some of the expenses incurred by the Phillipses? From 1973 to 1981 their joint income climbed from $27,500 to $57,000. The seven-and-a-half-year commuting costs of their marriage amounted to $40,450, which would average about $5,393 per year. They have spent $28,350 for air fares, $10,000 for furnishing a second house, $1,600 for long-distance phone calls, and $500 or so for extra clothing, since each needs a basic wardrobe in both places. With these high costs, why don't they just quit and get together? The problem is they have never been able to find acceptable jobs in the same vicinity. Interest in history is falling off among college students; so positions are impossible to find. Giving up an excellent job is a sacrifice neither wants to make. They both made stabs at career sacrifice. She went to San Diego with him at first and took a part-time instructorship at a San Diego evening college, but when she was offered the full-time position in Minnesota, an institution with a fine history department, she moved. When Carla moved, William took a year's unpaid leave and went to Minneapolis with her. He thought he could do research and that he might find a job in the area. In fact, he did get a position, but it was only a fill-in post for one year. When his leave was over, the couple took out Western Airlines credit cards and started the fortnightly shuttle. They cash in on cut-rate advance purchases and sometimes have as many as four round-trip tickets on hand, but their plane fares averaged $690 a month in 1981. The Phillipses have chosen not to have children on their salaries that offer few prospects for a dramatic rise in income. Salaries are eroded by commuting expenses, but they do have his-and-her condos. The interest and taxes on two houses allow them to claim additional deductions on income taxes. They don't receive a hefty refund, but they aren't lending money interest free to the government because they filed W-4 forms claiming these extra deductions.

Financial advisers suggested that they investigate limited partnerships, money-market funds, and tax-sheltered annuities as a means of making up some of the expenses of their long-distance marriage. The Phillipses always have investments on their minds because their double life makes it hard to save for an inflation-threatened future. One adviser suggested the unorthodox idea of a divorce as a way of saving on taxes. And it is true. The tax laws are so crazy that they still contain a built-in penalty for married people who both work, and filing separate returns as married individuals is not the same as filing individual single returns. Beginning with the 1982 tax return there was an effort to alleviate the marriage penalty with a special two-earner marriage deduction, but you shouldn't be fooled. The two-earner marriage penalty has not been eliminated. Even after the marriage deduction was fully phased in, it did not counteract the penalty built into the law. The tax laws therefore perpetuate the tradition of a single-earner household, and couples deviating from this norm are penalized. It is quite right that the financial situation of couples like the Phillipses would be improved if they divorced, in spite of the fact that their marriage is no part-time affair nor is it an "open" marriage (Seixas 1981:78).

The Phillipses aren't the only commuters to report money problems. Other couples also say that the dollar cost of split living adds to the problems of making it work. Elizabeth Burkhard, who was assistant deputy administrator of the Veterans Administration when she spoke about weekend marriage to the *Wall Street Journal* in 1981, said that long-distance phone bills of $50 to $75 a month were only the beginning. She flew every two or three weeks to her home in Houston and had booked plane reservations a year in advance to get the lower "supersaver" rate. She also bought a house in Washington and reported being so financially strapped that the house had to be furnished with items found at clearance sales and discount centers (Langley 1981).

One problem that was not expected by most couples is total confusion over finances. A couple married for 18 years commuting between Massachusetts and Washington, D.C., says, "It is hard to keep everything straight, trying to figure out who is writing what check and making sure there's no duplication. But we're getting squared away" (U.S. *News and World Report* 1977:110). Another couple, however, became so confused that the wife forgot to pay the husband's utility bill and his electricity was turned off.

Another costly item for commuters, especially those with children, is household help and household maintenance. There is not time to do it yourself. Dorothy M. Simon, a corporate vice president at Avco Corp. in Greenwich, Connecticut, says, "The first thing you have to do is get rid of the worries of taking care of multiple households. Get household help" (*Business Week* 1978:68). Other couples interviewed firmly agree. But this is possible only in situations where joint income is in the upper ranges. For example, take the case of John L. Sullivan, Jr., 49, an executive recruiter with Heidrick & Struggles Inc. in San Francisco and his wife, Barbara Byle Sullivan, 40, president of Boyle/Kirkman Associates, Inc., a New York management consulting firm specializing in affirmative action programs. This couple estimate that they spend $10,000 a year on air fares alone in order to get together on weekends and holidays. They believe it makes sense to use as many outside services as possible to protect the time they have together (*Business Week* 1978:68).

The $10,000 airfare may represent an upper level, but couples with joint incomes of between $20,000 and $30,000 report spending from $960 to $1,800 annually for travel between their two residences. But it seems the more money you have, the more practical a commuter marriage becomes, and the more likely this new style of living becomes as well. Transfers that can lead to two-city marriage are more likely when a career is highly successful, when children are older and no longer at home, and when the couple is highly affluent. The Etelsons are a good example. Doris Etelson, vice president of Howard Johnson Co., lives and works in the Boston area, but her husband, Robert, lives and works in Pomona, New York. Every weekend Doris drives or hops on a plane to visit Robert in Pomona. Twice a week, her husband takes a plane to spend the night in Boston.

Their heavy commuting schedule allows them to be together five days a week. "They have been able to keep to this tiring, expensive schedule because their children are in their twenties and are no longer at home, because Mr. Etelson has encouraged his wife's career, and because *they are a highly affluent couple"* (emphasis mine) (Gallese 1978:1).

The Affluent, the Political, and the Celebrated

The Etelsons report that living and working in different cities has produced few anxieties. In fact, Robert is enthusiastic about the arrangement because he believes the one-hour flight to Boston is a lot less taxing than the 70-mile drive from his office to his home. The couple feels that the arrangment has opened "a whole new vista" for both of them. He enjoys Boston and has a great time visiting shops and doing the local restaurants with Doris. He is not troubled by having an executive wife because he's satisfied with his own work with the air-freight company that he built. Doris, who began work with Howard Johnson in 1961, realized by the mid-seventies that her next move up would depend on her willingness to go where an executive job opened up, and that having to remain where her husband had his business was limiting her and therefore her value to her company. Her husband's cooperation, the fact that her children are now out of high school, and the high-salaried executive positions of the Etelsons make the two-city arrangement more desirable.

The most frequent negative response from commuters interviewed and surveyed was the money problem. Money is a great obstacle for commuters of middle-class status. Even though middle-income couples realize that they will never become independently wealthy engaging in commuter marriage, the expense when careers are just beginning is enormous. A good portion of couples' paychecks go for travel, telephone, and maintaining two homes. These are the basics. Extras will include dual wardrobes, household help, boarding schools or day care. According to previous research and information gathered from spouses in two-city marriages, the average family income for commuters is presently over $40,000 annually. It is an expensive lifestyle. The money bugaboo comes as a shock to some. Balancing the two checkbooks, finding new doctors and dentists, lugging prized silver or family heirlooms back and forth to have them on hand at both locations for parties can be trying. But in a time when divorce is becoming more and more common in the traditional comfort of a one-city home, commuters seem to be determined to bring off the new two-city arrangement.

The Downs are a marriage-on-the-wing couple who are making the expensive arrangement work. "Mary Downs, 38, is a Denver stockbroker who commutes to Washington, D.C., where her husband, Fred, 37, is a Veterans Administration official . . . she says, 'D.C. was dragging me down. I was a superbitch because I was unhappy about where I was living.' Now she is happily self-sufficient with good friends in both cities and reunions with Fred 'like honeymoons.' His male friends question the arrangement as friends and in-laws often do about commuting couples, managing to imply that the marriage is in trouble. Not so, says Mary. 'We have always had good communication—both cerebral and sexual—which encourages us that we are doing the right thing. We are still a couple'" (Leo 1982:83).

Affluent couples can make the very best of their two-city life. One couple, Marc and Lois Wyse, are one of the few who actually expect to straddle two cities permanently, and they have quite formal arrangments for making the situation enjoyable. He is the Cleveland-based president of an advertising agency, and she is the agency's New York–based vice president. Their sophisticated system for travel is based upon the season, and one is reminded of traditional, wealthy Spanish royalty who leave Madrid in the hot summer months for the cooler seasonal capital in San Sebastian. The Wyses spend every other weekend in the winter at their Manhattan brownstone, going to the theater and dining out. In summer they retreat to their suburban Cleveland home to enjoy the outdoors and the swimming pool (*Business Week* 1978:67). The formal, well-organized arrangements of the Wyses are more difficult to achieve in the hectic life of a political two-city marriage with one partner winging back and forth to Washington.

Washington, D.C., may indeed be the dual-residence mecca. Pendleton James, President Reagan's chief personal assistant, reported in 1981 that the commuting phenomenon was much more widespread than when he served in the Nixon White House a decade earlier. James reported that government posts present an alluring challenge and that more and more persons are willing to live apart to take advantage of what could be a fleeting opportunity (Langley 1981:1). The life is that of a workaholic: hectic, stressful, but very well paid. *Time* in 1982 noted that political commuters included Drew Lewis, Secretary of Transportation, and Marilyn Lewis, state legislator.

"The secret is to roll with the punches," says Lewis. "When the schedule changes, you've got to be totally flexible, whatever comes. Just don't worry about it." Lewis and his wife Marilyn, both 50, seem to spend their time in automobiles driving the triangle from their farm outside Philadelphia to Washington and Harrisburg where Marilyn is a second-term delegate in the state legislature. "I love all the driving," she says, "because it lets me collect my thoughts, and when I'm driving with Drew, it's a private time when the telephone doesn't ring." Drew grouses about the inconveniences—the right clothes are always in the wrong city and leisure activities are pared to the bone. Says he: "There isn't much time for fun things, but with Marilyn in the legislature, our conversation is much broader. We don't have to discuss the garden, the dog, and the children." (Leo 1982:83).

Other political commuters have included: Marjory Mecklenburg, an acting deputy assistant secretary of the Health and Human Services Department, who flew each week from Washington to Minneapolis where her physician husband lived; Barbara Thomas, Securities and Exchange Commissioner, whose husband was a New York attorney; Tim McNamar, deputy secretary of the Treasury, who commuted to California; Peter Libassi, former general counsel of the old Health, Education, and Welfare Department; Jerry Jordan, a member of the President's Council of Economic Advisers, who said he works, sleeps, and travels to New Mexico where his wife is a graduate student; Anne Jones, a Federal Communications Commission member, who noted that her husband wouldn't want her to do anything but seize a good opportunity; and Helen von Damm, President Reagan's personal secretary and presidential aide, married to

Byron Leeds, a New York business executive. Helen von Damm stated what most of the political and affluent commuters feel, that their careers are more of a commitment than a job. She said, "After working for the President for 15 years, I couldn't leave now when we got what we've worked for." (Langley 1981:20).

While academic couples manage to juggle commuting quite successfully on $40,000 to $50,000 family incomes, primarily because they have flexible work schedules, the celebrities often have both flexible work obligations and incomes in six figures to make commuting more comfortable and more practicable. Football pros, television anchor people, successful entrepreneurs, film stars, and the like frequently find long-distance marriage the answer to having both a career and a permanent relationship.

But Terry Bradshaw and JoJo Starbuck couldn't make it work even though their courtship had also been a long-distance affair, and money was certainly not a problem. The problem was that they came to marriage with vastly different expectations and were never able to work them out. Differences became a source of conflict. Terry said, "She is primarily show biz, ballet and classical music, while I'm cows and horses and country music." But above all Terry had the traditional notion that "I'll work and take care of her—my wife and I will be together." While he was looking for the supportive wife, she was bored with being home alone all day playing Suzy Homemaker and wanted instead to take advantage of the momentum that was building in her career (Kaplan 1979:40).

So although money helps, other factors can be far more important. One couple interviewed had a family income of only $25,000 and yet they reported that their two-city relationship was a good one. They had been caught in the most recent economic crisis when so many people were without jobs. The wife, Carey, 35, said, "Yes, commuter marriage has been good for us. For one thing, it beats unemployment checks, which would have caused tension. It is better than having a husband home 24 hours a day feeling depressed. I'd say what you have to do to make it work is to support each other. Show your husband you trust him and don't be jealous. I was familiar with my surroundings while he was not. Commuting was far harder on him." This couple estimate they limit commuting costs to about $40 per month—mostly in travel and telephone expense. Meanwhile, one of the affluent, Sunny Griffin, 37, beauty and fashion director for Avon Products, Inc., said in *Business Week* (1978:68), "If I ever saw a phone bill under $300, I considered that month's phone service free." Alberta Arthurs sums up the general feeling with: "You really have to love what you're doing to pay all the additional costs. There are no tax benefits whatsoever from this lifestyle."

Advice to the Tax Forlorn: Assertive Tax Management

"There is no tax advantage in a commuting marriage," says the IRS auditor as you sit alone at the hearing with your shoebox full of airline ticket stubs, telephone bills, mortgage payment receipts on two houses, and canceled checks. Well, half the canceled checks anyway—your spouse in Houston has the rest. The truth is, the Fagin sitting across from you is merely taking an assertive stance on behalf of the IRS, and you must be equally assertive in protecting your rights under the tax laws. Indeed, there is no direct tax advantage in a commuting marriage; so there is no point in telling the humorless Scrooge auditing you about the financial peril in which you live as a commuter. But neither do you have to roll over and bare your throat to the fangs of an increasingly greedy tax system. You won't get automatic deductions for a commuter lifestyle, and most accountants will not have the information about your tax situation to help you make the best of it when you file your return on April 15 or when you must go for an audit triggered by the deductions of your unusual lifestyle. "I have been audited five times in the past eight years," says one two-city wife, "but I have never had to pay an extra dime. In fact, on every occasion I found additional deductions when audited and actually got another refund." Don't panic! There's a lot you can do to help your tax situation, but there's also a lot you won't be able to do—or at best you must be very careful about doing. The short form is out. If you want any break at all, you'll have to do a full long 1040.

The first suggestion is to live the way you want to live but keep good records. It's difficult in the hectic commuting situation, but if you have good records of what you have spent, you'll find that there may be all kinds of deductions you can take that you never before dreamed of. You gather your records in two ways. First, in an expense journal—preferably one of those page-a-day books that are usually used for appointments. You can write down everything you do, where you are, whom you've seen, with whom you had lunch or dinner. In the extra space you can make notes on what went on in those meetings. The only other thing you need to do for record keeping is save receipts— for everything. A great nuisance, admittedly, but worth it in the long run. It goes without saying that canceled checks are saved too. If you have trouble keeping all this stuff, there are filing systems available in office supply stores that can help; accordion folding files that bulge nicely by the end of the tax year, series of large labeled envelopes, loose-leaf books with handy pockets. And, if you get really involved in assertive tax management you can use your computer for most of it. Another way to handle those receipts is to simply toss them *all* into a drawer. Then sometime before April 15, the whole thing is emptied out and sorted into appropriate tax categories.

Your journal can serve as a backup system to help you remember what otherwise might slip your mind. Or, if you've been careless and forgotten to keep receipts in your on-the-wing lifestyle, your journal can substantiate your expenditures. For instance, let's suppose you are an accountant and you periodically join a group of other accountants for luncheons held at local restaurants, or that you sometimes take a client to lunch. At these luncheons you discuss the latest professional journals you have read, or you talk about computerized accounting, or you discuss clients' problems. If the lunch or dinner meeting is sufficiently business related, the full cost is deductible. Should you forget to ask for a receipt, it is still deductible if in your journal you record in a timely manner (which means that day or early the next) the following information:

1. The *amount* of each separate item (can include telephone calls and taxi fares as well as food);
2. The *date* of the expense (you'll have it right there on the journal page);
3. The *place* of entertainment or expenditure;
4. The business *purpose*;
5. The occupation of or other information concerning the person you met with or entertained (including name, title, business relationship to you).

Your expense journal is also required for travel deductions, and in some cases it can be used to establish reasonable amounts even if your required receipts are missing. This doesn't mean you should ignore receipt keeping, but in the long run, your expense journal can be more important. Write in it the DDAP for each trip or entertainment. DDAP is the key word that will help you remember to list the *date, destination, amount, purpose.* You'll never be caught unaware by an audit, and you won't forget that business lunch with Laura or the shuttle to Washington at 2:00 P.M. on March 21.

What if you didn't keep records? You can still deduct your expenses—even if you're audited. If you can establish that you are entitled to a certain business deduction, you may be allowed to estimate your actual expense in the absence of records under what is called the Cohan Rule. You can bet that you'll have to agree to a low estimate, however, so it's best to begin keeping records even if you haven't done so in the past. You'll need every tax advantage you can think of in a long-distance marriage arrangement. These are some of the things you can keep in mind not just as April 15 approaches, but all year long.

Housing. As a dual-residence family, you can't deduct the money spent for maintaining two households or for any air or auto travel. But, like the Phillipses mentioned above, you *can* deduct the interest and taxes on two houses if you own them, and this will allow you to claim additional deductions on your

W-4 forms. The IRS then will not withhold so much tax from your income each month. A rough and probably low estimate of interest and taxes for two medium-priced condos might be about $9,000 a year. As a married couple you are allowed $3,400 as your zero-bracket deduction; so your interest and taxes alone are the equivalent of about five additional exemptions ($5,600). Assuming you're in the 43 percent bracket, you would take home an extra $2,000 during the year. Naturally, you won't get the hefty refund after April 15 that you would have without these extra deductions, but you'll have extra income each paycheck to put into a money-market fund, an IRA, a tax-sheltered annuity, or maybe even a limited partnership which would give you additional tax write-offs for depreciation and expenses.

The question of joint tenancy versus individual ownership of houses is a complicated one. For married couples filing a joint return, it makes no tax difference whether a house or other assets are owned jointly or individually by either spouse. But it can make a difference when property is sold or when it is transferred after the death of one spouse. It can also make a difference if you decide it could be an advantage to file separate tax returns. The major situation where separate returns may be better is in the case where both of you have capital gains or losses produced by property owned individually, or in some cases where one person sustains very high medical expenses.

In many states, filing a joint return can be idiotic because the same rate schedule is used for joint state tax returns as for single returns. In this situation filing a joint return can cost you money because it shifts income from a smaller bracket to a higher bracket. Be sure to check whether the joint return rate is the same as the separate return rate in your state. You can save literally hundreds of dollars by *not* filing a joint return. Commuting couples should seek professional advice on how various forms of ownership can affect their tax situations and on how renting their larger family-size home that may not be needed can help.

You can even rent your home to your spouse. Under a surprising loophole, rental to a family member or a co-owner is not considered personal use, provided that a fair market rental is charged and the dwelling is the principal residence of the person to whom it is rented. If the individual's "own use" does not exceed the 15 day/10 percent limit, all allowable rental expenses, including depreciation (furniture depreciation as well), can be deducted even if this produces a loss. The 15 day/10 percent limit means that you can't use the home for the greater of either 15 days or 10 percent of the number of days during the year that the home is rented out. For example, if you rent to your spouse for 10 months you could use the home 30 days (10 percent of 300 days). However, if the home is rented for 12 consecutive months, this restriction doesn't apply. You have to report the rent as income, but you can deduct all kinds of expenses associated with renting, maybe even the new carpet and bathroom fixtures. It's worth checking into if you live in two locations anyway. If you do it right, you can even rent to each other.

Travel. The sticky thing for commuters is the enormous travel expense. Can anything be done about it? Isn't there some way to recover at least a portion? Maybe so. The thing to remember is to try and convert some of this travel into business travel. The Phillipses are doing this by writing a book together. It is perfectly legitimate to get together to collaborate on a book or some other project connected with business or professions. At least some trips can be written off this way if indeed you are actively collaborating. Try this—invite members of a professional organization, service club, or society to hear your spouse speak on a topic of interest to the group. By sharing your partner's expertise, you can write the weekend trip off as business expense and maybe even write off the refreshments served and meals as well.

Robert, 48, who is a professor of education at an eastern college, says, "The first year we commuted between West Virginia and Colorado we were able to deduct expenses for four round trips. First, I was invited by Mary's institution to give a series of lectures, and then she came here to do a week's workshop on multicultural education. Next, we both applied to present papers at a professional conference in Pennsylvania. The papers were accepted; so we spent a week together on neutral turf at a resort where the conference was being held. Then we developed a summer exchange program between students on her campus and students here in West Virginia. We needed a tax-deductible trip to make the final plans for the exchange and to write a proposal to fund the program. With this joint professional activity, we were able to write off some of our telephone expense that was business connected. Our phone bills had been averaging about $200 per month. We cut those bills somewhat by using professional credit card numbers for business-related calls." Robert and Mary would have been working together on some of these activities if they lived in the same city. The two-city situation simply allowed them the opportunity to get travel expenses that were deductible. Couples in other professions can adapt these ideas to their own career situations. The only necessary ingredient is creative tax planning. How can you and your spouse legitimately spend time together and use this time and travel as a business expense?

If you decide to meet at a business conference or professional meeting, you can get a tax break even when only one partner is involved in the meeting. Ordinarily, when you travel for professional reasons accompanied by your spouse or other family members, their expenses are not deductible. However, if your spouse meets you at a conference or some other travel-related business activity, you do not have to split your expenses down the middle. For example, you may deduct $75 for lodging when a single room costs $75 even though you occupy a double room for $85 because your spouse is along. The nondeductible cost is only $10, and you've had a romantic rendezvous almost free. When you dine out, make sure the wine and expensive appetizers are on the bill that is business-related. The commuter lifestyle is not without cost, but it has its advantages.

There is nothing sinful about combining travel-for-business and travel-for-pleasure. Whether a trip is primarily for business or primarily for pleasure depends on the facts in each case. However, the length of time spent in business or in personal activities is an important factor. If the trip is primarily for business or related to your profession, it is deductible. A commuting couple can win thousands of dollars in tax deductions if they plan their trips properly. For example, Mary attends the annual convention of the American Chemical Society in San Diego. She stays at the convention for five days and spends most of her time attending sessions of the convention. Maybe she takes the Tijuana Trolly across the border for some incidental sightseeing, but for the most part she listens to papers presented by society members. At the end of the conference instead of going directly back to St. Louis, she flies to San Francisco to visit her husband for a day before returning from there to her home in Missouri. Mary can claim that the trip was primarily a business trip to attend the convention. The side trip to San Francisco was not her primary purpose. Mary can deduct her food and lodging expenses in San Diego and what the cost of transportation *would* have been had she flown directly between St. Louis and San Diego. She can't deduct expenses incurred while in San Francisco with her husband, but she has made the trip there almost totally tax deductible.

Combining business with pleasure travel outside the United States is somewhat different. You must meet a number of conditions. Normally you must be outside the U.S. a week or less; you must have received a travel expense allowance from your employer; you must spend 75 percent of the total time outside the U.S. on business activities; you must show you had no substantial control over arranging the trip. Meeting all these conditions sounds like a formidable task, but don't despair. Sometimes, it is possible to convert a trip originally motivated by personal considerations into a deductible business trip. Remember the Phillipses? They spend their summers in Spain doing research for their book—in dusty libraries some of the time, but the trip is a legitimate expense. All you need to do is to *allocate expenses* if you don't meet all the conditions listed above. This means you divide the expenses between business and nonbusiness activities.

The formula is quite simple. For example, your spring trip to the Netherlands. You leave New York for Amsterdam on Wednesday and return on Friday of the following week (10 days). Your presence is required for a specific business purpose on five days. They need not be full work days; in fact, you could have spent most of your time tiptoeing through the tulips with your spouse, but you had to be at those meetings from 9 to 10 A.M. Weekends are also counted as business days because you're on standby for the meeting on Monday. Therefore, you can count seven business days and three nonbusiness days. You figure it this way.

nonbusiness days times airline round trip fare
(3 × $1,000 = $3,000)
$3,000 divided by total days outside U.S.
($3,000 ÷ 10 = $300)

You find that $300 of your airfare is not deductible—$700 then *is* deductible. You can also deduct all your expenses for lodging and meals for seven days. Roughly then, something over two-thirds of your trip is a legitimate tax expense; so you have your interlude in Amsterdam for a bargain rate. If both of you can find business reasons for your travel, it becomes more of a bargain.

Children. Expensive as they are, children can also help you save money on taxes. The basic principle is simple. You are in a certain tax bracket and your child is in a lower (usually zero) tax bracket. If you can shift some of your income from yourself to your child, then you will have reduced or eliminated altogether the income tax due on such amounts. Amounts shifted to children can be saved to provide them with, in effect, a tax-free education, or a tax-free allowance, or extras like music lessons or summer camp. You can't shift income earned as a salary, but income on investments such as stocks, bonds, savings accounts, and royalties can be shifted. In order to shift the tax burden, you must also transfer the property which produces the income, at least temporarily. The Uniform Gifts to Minors Act provides a simple way to transfer securities, life insurance policies, or money to a minor and still retain the power to buy, sell, and reinvest these items on behalf of the minor child. You or your spouse can be declared custodian.

Recent court decisions have also allowed you to use no-interest loans for income shifting. For instance, Tommy, Jr., is in a lower tax bracket than his dad, Thomas, Sr.; so dad makes a no-interest loan to Tommy of his invested funds on which he is earning an income. Since Tommy is in a zero tax bracket, a net tax reduction is achieved. The loan has no fixed expiration date, but rather is a payable-on-demand note. This means that dad has the privilege of recalling the loan and getting his original funds back at any time he chooses. Because the donor will be getting the original funds back, only the income on these funds is being shifted to Tommy. No-interest loans are simpler and more flexible than short-term trusts. There is no 10-year restriction as on short-term trusts, and the length of time the arrangement is in force doesn't have to be stated in advance. One parent can act as custodian to establish a legally enforceable obligation to repay the loan by the minor child. The IRS is trying to nip this tax twist in a new law, but exceptions for certain loans may still be available.

Another way to lower taxes due on income produced by a business you might own is to pay your children for assisting you. You get a deduction for the wages you pay them, while they generally pay no tax on the amounts received because of the $1,000 personal exemption and the $2,300 standard deduction to which they are entitled. The salary you pay your minor child is also exempt from social security tax and unemployment insurance, but the salary must be in actual wages and not room and board. Since payments made to a child have a very real potential for abuse, the IRS sometimes takes a skeptical view. If you keep suitable records and the payments are made in a businesslike manner, the deduction *will* hold up even if the child is only 7 years old and answers the phone or does ground maintenance. Ordinarily a single person (including a child)— will pay no tax on the first $3,300 earned.

Children also allow you to qualify for a tax credit equal to a percentage of payments made to a babysitter, maid, housekeeper, day care center, nursery school, summmer camp, etc. The exact percentage you may deduct depends upon your adjusted gross income. The credit for household services and child care is subtracted directly from your final tax liability instead of from taxable income; so it is more valuable to you than a deduction of the same amount, such as interest on a house payment, medical expenses, or deductions for books, professional dues, and so forth. Commuters with children almost always qualify for this tax credit. Three rules have to be satisfied. First, your expenses must be necessary to enable you to be gainfully employed (or you could be actively looking for employment). Second, you must have a dependent under age 15 or a disabled dependent over 14; and finally your payment for the service can't be made to a child of yours under age 19 or to a person who is claimed as your dependent. This last would allow you to hire the children's grandparents; so you can transfer money to relatives this way and achieve a net reduction in tax, usually without increasing the person's income tax.

Some of the child care items you can write off as a tax credit include:

1. *Expenses within the home* necessary to the home for the well-being of the child. This includes a housekeeper, maid, babysitter, but not a gardener. Cost of meals for household help also qualify, and a maid or housekeeper is not required to have any direct child care responsibilities.

2. *Expenses outside the home* such as day camp, nursery school, day care centers including meals. One hitch, though: private school tuition for a child in the first or higher grades may not qualify. But summer camp for these older children could indeed qualify, and recently court cases are supporting your right to a child care tax credit for a portion of the expenses you incur for private school. If you want to try it, you must be very sure that you can support the fact that you *could not* have accepted your job without having sent the child to the boarding or private school. An example would be a situation where the public school classroom was fraught with disorders, teacher strikes, gang fights, or the like, and you could not work while your child attended the school because you had to remain constantly prepared to pick the child up if problems arose.

The amount of tax credit is dependent on adjusted gross income. In 1984 you could take 30 percent of expenses on adjusted income up to $10,000. From there the percentage decreases step by step until it reaches 20 percent for incomes of $28,001 and over, and there is a maximum limitation of $2,400 if there is one qualifying dependent or $4,800 if there are two or more qualifying dependents. One other tricky point—the expenses cannot exceed either your earned income or your spouse's earned income—whichever is *lower*. Therefore, in some cases, it pays to "put a spouse on the payroll" in some fashion in order to boost the earned income of the lower-earning spouse and obtain the higher tax credit.

Books, Supplies, and Equipment Deductions. It is easy to forget some of these small items, but you are entitled to a deduction for the cost of books, periodicals, supplies, equipment, home computers, and other items you use in your profession or for business purposes. Items that have a short lifespan such as paper or pencils are deducted fully in the year they are purchased. Computers, desks, and books can be deducted with one or two options: the expensing option and the depreciation option.

Under the expensing option you simply deduct the cost of the items up to a total deduction of $5,000 in the year they are put into use. Under the depreciation option a specified percentage of the cost is deducted in every year of the depreciation period. Books, equipment, and furniture have a depreciation period of 5 years. Automobiles, light trucks, and some research equipment have a depreciation period of 3 years. Other items such as houses, apartments, and other buildings (not land) have a 15-year depreciation. The reason that the depreciation option might be used instead of the expensing option is that an extra investment credit can be claimed under the depreciation. Any good tax book can tell you how to do these fancy depreciation and investment tax credit maneuvers. Just remember, don't forget the small things such as professional books (not such a small expense anymore), periodicals connected with your job, supplies of all kinds down to the last paper clip, and even your newspapers and magazines, which can be deductible if they are connected with your job. A public relations executive bought *Time* and *Newsweek* and purchased newspapers and other magazines, stating that they were needed by him in connection with his work. He didn't even keep a record of his purchases but estimated his expense and the Small Tax Court allowed the deduction. The Small Tax Court also allowed a teacher $125 for miscellaneous educational supplies even though the teacher had no documentation.

Be careful on the home computer deduction, though. If you use it for Jungle Hunt, Zork, or Caves of Adelphi, you're not entitled to deduct that percentage of the computer that is used for these personal purposes. Make sure to avoid suspicion by having the game cartridges listed on a separate invoice—not with your basic equipment and software. The IRS isn't going to like your home computer deduction. To protect it you will have to be sure you can demonstrate that the equipment is absolutely required for your job or investments.

Living in Sin. When all else fails you can live in sin and avoid the "marriage penalty." The history of this tax on marriage is farcical, except that it is costly. The whole thing started with the community property law which said that half of a "man's" income really belongs to his wife. The concept began with the Visigoths. By their seventh-century law, all plunder from war had to be divided equally between husband and wife. In the twentieth century the paycheck takes the place of plunder, and we have the idea of community property. But not all states had community property laws, and in the community property states men with large incomes could avoid the high tax rates imposed on those in upper brackets by splitting the income with their wives. These families then dropped down to the tax bracket of half their income. The rich in other states began to complain; so in 1948 Congress allowed all married couples regardless of where they lived to split their incomes. And then the single people became envious and complained. In 1969 Congress listened to them and gave them relief by reducing the rate for single individuals. No one noticed it at the time, but the new low rates for singles meant that a working couple who married found themselves paying more income tax between them than the sum total of what they had paid as single persons. Now all the married people began to howl because they were penalized for their morality whenever the lower-income spouse earned about 25 percent as much as the higher-income spouse. They attacked the law as an encouragement to immorality. Finally

President Carter asked Congress to change the law to curb the tax advantage of "living in sin."

Also contributing to the marriage penalty are numerous provisions that limit the various deductions and credits that can be claimed by married couples, more severely than would be the case if the couple were unmarried: for example, the limits on moving expenses and child care. To give some relief from the marriage penalty, Congress has instituted a special deduction which can be claimed by two-earner couples who file joint returns. This special deduction went into effect on 1982 tax returns and was equal to 5 percent of the qualified earned income of the spouse with the *lower* income up to a maximum of $1,500. For 1983 and later years, the 5 percent/$1,500 figures are doubled to 10 percent and $3,000. The IRS reports that in 1983 many couples failed to take full advantage of this new tax break. Don't be one of them!

But has the marriage penalty been eliminated? Not at all. Even now that the two-earner marriage deduction is fully phased in, it will not counteract the marriage penalty. An exact comparison depends on the breakdown of a married couple's income and deductions. If you do qualify for the two-earner deduction, though, you should adjust the amount being withheld from your paychecks accordingly. You can do this by filing a W-4 form. The marriage deduction is claimed on line 29 of Form 1040 as an adjustment to inome. For some long-distance couples in the middle income brackets the marriage penalty has been reduced to about one-third of what it was under the old law, but for others, the deduction will be much less effective. In cases where there is considerable income from pensions, interest, dividends, investment income, and other things excluded from "earned income," couples will still find that living in sin remains a more effective way to reduce taxes than the marriage deduction.

Temporary Jobs Away From Home. As a two-location couple you each have what the IRS calls a separate "tax home." "Home" has a special meaning to the IRS, and it's not at all sentimental. Home means specifically the general area of your principal place of employment, regardless of where you maintain your "family residence." Even if you both lived in Chicago but worked in Milwaukee, your tax home would be Milwaukee, and if you stay there overnight you are not considered to be away from home overnight. So you can't deduct the cost of commuting between your spouse's residence and your work. The only exceptions to this are business trips and temporary business locations; so the "temporary job away from home" *can* be explored. To qualify the job must be temporary in the eyes of the law. This means that at the time you start, the job must be foreseen to end within a fixed and reasonably short time. The IRS takes the approach that a short time is one year. But if your case is challenged because you've had a temporary job for 16 months, hold firm and appeal the audit because in many cases IRS policy has been overruled. The temporary job situation is complex. Three common threads are: first, the job must indeed be temporary; second, there must be significant ties to the worker's home base (family bonds or financial bonds); and third, the tax court refers back to the original reason for permitting a person at a temporary position away from home to deduct living expenses—*to provide relief to someone incurring duplicate expenses at two different locations.* Since living expenses at a position away from home are very large, as all commuter couples know, if there is a reasonably legitimate way to deduct these expenses it is well worth the try. If you *can* meet the conditions, you will be allowed to deduct the cost of meals, lodging, cleaning and laundry, and commuting. The separate "tax home" interpretation by the IRS may soon be questioned. At present it's difficult to get around, but commuter couples are indeed suffering extra expenses. They certainly meet the test of "suffering extra expenses" that the tax court places so much emphasis on. Perhaps it is time for some test cases to complain loudly, as did the married folk back in 1948 and the single folk back in 1969. Tax laws can be changed. It's done all the time. Maybe it's time for commuter couples to begin to howl.

Pointers for Minimizing Taxes. For two-career couples with separate and permanent places of employment, it is difficult to get around the separate "tax home" situation. So far, the law provides no deductions especially designed for two-paycheck households, and certainly it provides nothing specifically for two-paycheck, two-residence households. However, existing regulations affect you as a commuter couple in a number of ways. Take advantage of what you can by being an assertive, creative taxpayer who keeps good records and keeps up on the frequent changes in the law. Briefly, keep these things in mind.

- In most cases you won't save by using the "married, filing separately" option.
- Housing should be carefully thought out so that you can either take whopping interest deductions on two homes or rent to each other.
- All your travel should be documented with the DDAP method explained above to insure that you won't forget travel items and so you have records should you be audited. Be creative about planning where you'll go for business and professional meetings; maybe you can get together and write off at least part of the expenses. Remember, travel for business can be travel for pleasure.
- Having children can allow you to take tax credit for child care, but this child care can also involve a maid or housekeeper. Children can reduce your taxable income by allowing you to shift some of your money to their zero bracket. You can also pay your child a salary.
- Remember the little things, such as books, supplies, equipment, computers, and the business dinners, lunches, and meetings you attend.
- Maybe you can arrange for your employment to be "temporary." You'd then be able to take enormous deductions for meals, lodging, cleaning, and commuting.
- Divorce and live in sin: the last resort and not so effective as it was before some relief was given to offset the marriage penalty.
- Get political. Tax laws can be changed. You do indeed suffer extra expenses. Commuter couples are becoming a significant minority as more wives become a permanent part of the work force.

Chapter Seven

"To Have and to Hold From This Day Forward . . ."

What Are Your Chances?

By 1990 it is conservatively estimated that 52 million women or 60 percent of the female population over 16 will be in the work force. There will be a higher family income, but less time to enjoy it. One in four U.S. households will have integrated video terminals and information systems. With a greater number of women having spent considerable time in jobs outside the home, a greater number will be deeply committed to their careers and employed in managerial and administrative jobs. While female managers increased by a mere 1 percent per decade from 1950 to 1970, there was an 8 percent increase from 1970 to 1979 according to the Bureau of Labor Statistics. Because managerial and administrative positions generally require greater geographical mobility, it is highly likely that the number of commuter marriages will increase. All research and economic evidence supports this position. The nature of work is changing. It is less physical, less dirty, less traditionally masculine. Women who go to work temporarily to ease a family financial crisis will find themselves working for longer periods. The advent of a high technological society where most jobs require years of formal training makes it less likely that women will give it all up and get back to the kitchen. Temporary situations tend to become permanent lifestyles, and commuter marriage, seen at present as an interim solution, may become permanent and widespread.

There is a very real expectation on the part of men that their wives will be employed. The time is upon us when there is to be a fuller sharing of work and domestic roles. Women want this—so do men. Men are asking, "Why can't I become involved in the care of my children without being considered a weirdo?" Women are asking, "Why can't I have a career without feeling guilty?" The dual-career family is said to be the most important social change of the twentieth century, and commuter marriage springs from this momentous alteration in the social structure.

Commuter marriage, like any relationship, can indeed be stressful, but it is not like the separation of traumatic circumstances such as imprisonment, war, or migration. Commuter couples are coming not from difficulties but from success in the late-twentieth-century high-tech world. The dual-residence lifestyle is a developing and possibly permanent solution for two-career couples because it doesn't require a forced choice between a job and an intimate relationship. Anyone can successfully participate in a two-city marriage. It is like the story told by an out-in-front editor of a large publishing house who had a two-year commuter relationship that was going great. She likened the concern about commuter marriage success to what had happened when she placed a close relative in a nursing home. She and her husband were concerned about how the elderly relative would respond to the new environment. Would the transition be a success, or a disaster? They were riddled with guilt and looking for reassurance that they were doing the right thing. They questioned the staff at the nursing home and finally received what they thought a sensible, realistic reply. "If your mother has been a happy person all her life, she will be happy here. If she has been a whiner and a complainer, she'll whine and complain here. The situation is not going to make any basic difference in her personality or behavior. She is the kind of person she is, and she'll be that person here in this new environment."

Commuters too are the kinds of persons they are, and they'll be that way whether living together seven days a week or only two or three. The ambitious remain ambitious. The chasers keep chasing. Those who are dependent remain dependent. But the following questionnaire and the explanation of responses that follows is designed to alert readers to some of the problems that others commuters have encountered. You can test yourself, and be forewarned about situations you might find perplexing or difficult.

To Commute or Not To Commute?

By answering these questions you will be able to get further acquainted with your own response to a commuter marriage. Circle the answer you feel most nearly describes your situation. Then turn to the explanations that follow. You will see what your strong points may be and what you should be cautious about.

1. Are you a woman or a man?
   man   woman

2. Rate *your* career motivation and aspirations.
   extremely high   high   moderate   average

3. Rate your *spouse's* career motivation and aspirations.
   extremely high   high   moderate   average

4. Rate *your* feelings toward the family or intimacy relationship.
   extremely important   important   moderate   average

5. Rate your *spouse's* feelings toward the family or intimacy relationship.
   extremely important   important   moderate   average

6. Will your two salaries offset added costs for housing, transportation, telephone bills?
   plenty left over   easily   barely   none left over

7. Does the husband accept his wife's career as important?
   fully accepting   accepting   says it's okay   no comment

8. How many miles do you or will you have to travel?
   1,000–2,000   500–1,000   250–500   50–250

9. How old are you?
   60–75   45–59   30–44   less than 30

10. How long have you been married?
    20 years +   12–20 years   6–12 years   − 6 years

11. Rate your energy level?
    dynamo   atomic   subatomic   fizzle

12. Rate your sense of humor?
    madcap   frolicsome   lighthearted   operatic

13. How do you manage your time?
    always organize   regularly organize   rarely organize   chaos

14. Does your work situation allow you flexibility?
    set my own hours   work a short week   punch a time clock

15. How frequently do you delegate tasks at home?
    every chance possible   sometimes   seldom   never

16. How frequently do you delegate tasks at work?
    every chance possible   sometimes   seldom   never

17. Do you enjoy problem-solving and decision-making?
    love the power   leave it to others   would rather not

18. How many leisure interests do you and your spouse have in common?
    four   two   one   none

19. Are you bothered by the opinions and attitudes of others?
    plenty   frequently   sometimes   never

20. Would you be resentful if you had to spend your birthday alone?
    mad as a hornet   angry   not important

21. Do you worry about infidelity?
    completely trusting   never worry   I worry   no trust

22. Does at least one of you have an established career?
    both established   one established   neither established

23. Have your companies responded in any way to your situation?
    positively   offered help   no response   negative response

24. How many children do you have?
    5 or more   3–4   1–2   none

25. How old are they?
    out of high school   secondary school
    elementary school   pre-school

Explanation of Responses

Woman or Man? (Question 1). All reports from commuter couples and all research information clearly shows that a wife will have an easier time with the commuter lifestyles than will her husband. Men are faced with the unmacho image if they allow their wives to go off without them or if they go off and are not followed by a trailing spouse. "It is unmanly to let your wife do that" is what men are told. Furthermore, the psychic stress for husbands may be greater because while she has something more, something special, he feels he has something less. He's lost the inalienable right of the male breadwinner to be the only career-oriented member of the family. Men can very much miss being in "first place," and having the only career that really counts. They're caught in a dilemma because they truly, fully want the development of their wives' professional lives, and so they can't openly express their resentment at losing the special position as head-of-household. To top off his situation and make matters more difficult for males, male support networks are not arranged for married singles. They're supposed to have a supportive wife beside them at social and business functions, or they're supposed to be on-the-make "swingin' hunks." Since commuter husbands fit into neither category, there is nowhere to go.

Certainly female commuters have problems too. They become pariahs with their more traditional female relatives and friends, and Hester Prynne to some male acquaintances and employers. Wives feel guilty because other husbands have the conventional one-career two-people support system. But overall, women are better able to cope with the long-distance situation—perhaps because they have so recently come into their own that they are full of courage and enthusiasm, but also because they have a firmer support system with other women and society at large that is a legacy elaborated slowly and sometimes painfully over the past two-and-a-half decades of the feminist movement. The two-location family is female determined and leaves the male as a renewed single in his established network at home or as a married single in a new location. In

both work and an intimate relationship having high importance, there is a type of built-in counseling where the couples seek out each other's advice, thereby enriching the relationship.

Cost of Living Together, Apart (Question 6). It is more comfortable to live in his-and-hers condos than it is to live in a small travel trailer while your spouse is in the comfortable family home. There can be more communication when you can pick up the phone without dreading the next bill. It is easier to maintain an intimacy relationship when you see each other every week rather than every other month because of high travel costs. It is more enjoyable to have a commuter marriage when the personnel policies and practices of the organization you work for are adequate to meet the needs and problems you have as a commuter family. It's not enough to hear that "Business firms are sooner or later going to have to change many personnel policies if they want to compete to hire bright men and women" (Maynard and Zawacki 1979:470). Sooner or later may be too late for you.

If money is going to be a problem in your commuter relationship, it is going to increase the stress. Many couples successfully continue commuting when there is no money left over after paying for the added costs of housing, transportation, and telephone bills, but those that are commuting with plenty left over are able to avoid many problems and enjoy the unique situation. If your salaries are adequate to meet expenses with at least a little remaining, it is easier to face the liabilities of loneliness and friends and associates who frequently feel awkward in a social situation with only one-half of a couple. Your romantic honeymoon weekends can be more romantic at a five-star restaurant than they are at Wendy's. At the very least, you won't have to spend so much time and energy being creative to achieve that same effect.

Husband's Acceptance of Wife's Career (Question 7). "Based strictly on our salaries, my wife makes more money than I do," said one professional man, "but neither of us thinks of it that way. We each contribute in our own ways, and whatever either of us does, it's done for both of us." If you become competitive and set up rivalries with your mate, you're in trouble. Money is one of the chief areas of rivalry, especially when her money begins to approach his earnings. It's then much harder for a man to be accepting of his wife's career. It's another thing that adds to the unmacho image of the commuter husband. Older males have less difficulty with acceptance of the wife's career aspirations and her success. If the husband is well established in his career, he can more readily say "It's her turn now." His competence has already been confirmed; he can assume the role of mentor and avoid rivalries. Successful commuters confess that they have outgrown the need to compete. "If Wally makes more money, I can have my greenhouse sooner. If I make more, he can have his Mercedes," said an attorney who thrives on competition outside her marriage. "Psychological warfare" games are out. Ego support can't be obtained at the cost of the wife's career aspirations. A suggestion from commuters says, "It's best to avoid categorizing household chores as man's work or women's work." Most prefer not to assign tasks. If one of you does the cooking, the other can clean up. The important thing is getting domestic things done, so that you can have the time for each other—not dominance conflicts.

How Far Do You Travel? (Question 8). The sheer degree of separateness may be a factor in generating a negative reaction to the pattern of commuter marriage. Agnes Farris (1978:104) who studied commuting while at the Sloan School of Management at MIT, noted that couples who commute on a monthly basis expressed dissatisfaction with the arrangement's effect on their marital relationship, while none of the couples who commute on a weekly basis expressed dissatisfaction. She suggested that dissatisfaction probably increases with the duration of separation, but that different couples can have different tolerances, or cut-off points, beyond which they experience stress. Farris isn't quite sure about the effect of distance. She remarks, "I noticed that while some people indicated in the interviews that they are paying a very high emotional price for their careers, others did not seem to attach great importance in their self-conception to being *together* as part of a close couple with daily interaction.

Career opportunities seemed to be more important" (emphasis is mine).

Meanwhile, Philip Blumstein and Pepper Schwartz (1983) in their investigation of American couples seemed to find that spending enough time together is the key for a healthy relationship. Like so many others, they place an emphasis on quantity of time rather than quality. But Larry McMurtry (1983:4), the novelist and screenwriter, in a discussion on loneliness takes the position that loneliness is intensified mainly by failed expectations. When things simply haven't turned out the way we want, or the way it's "spozed to be," loneliness deepens. When the "Prince Charming" has never arrived to carry us off to cared-for comfort or when the "little woman" is not there with the frilly apron and iced cocktail to sooth our woes, expectations fail. The wider the gap between the fantasy and reality, the greater the loneliness, and for commuters there is a chasm between cultural expectations and the reality of existence. This may be a greater factor than actual physical distance. But, be forewarned if you're 2,000 miles apart—it won't be like the suburbs. It could be better!

Your Age and Length of Marriage (Question 9–10). The stresses and joys of commuter marriage appear to be different for different age groups. The major difficulty for younger two-city couples is career conflict. Whose career should take precedence? Husbands may resent not being considered in "first place." If the wife's career is highly successful, the couple may find they are victims of the "hidden paycheck syndrome." Wives feel guilty because they have something extra by working outside the home. Violation of the unwritten marriage rules creates tension. Younger couples lack the shared years of experience, and they have not yet confirmed their career competence. However, they can more easily overcome negative pressure from friends and relatives because they seek friendships with singles or other commuters more readily than older couples.

The major problems of older, more established couples are associated with shifts in parental responsibility, especially when the children remain with the husband. Stresses for these couples may come in the form of the "identity syndrome," where conflicts center around whether one is being a good man or a good woman or even a good couple. When children remain with the mother, she may fall prey to the "intermittent husband syndrome." The more she is a supermom, the greater her difficulty in weekend role transition. The reverse happens, of course, when the children remain with the father. The intermittent wife returns, reasserts her position as mother without success, and becomes resentful when she finds herself a "second parent."

Overall, it appears that the problems of younger couples may cause greater tension. Couples in their late 30s or older who have been married more than thirteen years usually have an easier time of it. The lack of outside friendships can create difficulties, though. With time so filled with successful careers and their relationship, the established couples often isolate themselves from the outsiders who can provide a support system. If at least one partner has already "arrived" and competence is confirmed, the arrangement goes more smoothly.

A surprising number of successful two-city couples seem to be in second marriages that have lasted more than ten years. The longer the marriage, the easier coping with two cities seems to be. Seven years of marriage before commuting seem to make things go better. Years give solidarity and shared emotional experience plus the faith that you can endure the demands of living apart.

Your Energy Level (Question 11). Two-location marriage is tiring. You can, however, turn the reunions into a new courtship. Commuters say it is great fun, but requires a reservoir of energy. Sometimes the romantic fantasies of wild sexual bouts turn into bed weariness, and the most amorous thing you can do is snuggle together. A precondition for dual-career marriage is a relatively high energy level because so very much involved is contrary to custom. You can't simply slide by; being unconventional requires extra energy, mental and physical. But if the dual-career couple can get along at the "atomic" level of energy, the dual-residence couple needs a "dynamo" rating because in this arrangement spouses have gone beyond the unusual to the downright eccentric. There are very few external supportive institutions to help, and this means that if the commuter marriage is to work, a great deal will depend upon the individuals' sheer persistence, drive, and energy supply. Mary Maples (1981:21) suggests that physical fitness should be included in the composite of what characterizes couples in this unusual arrangement. And what most report is that they do indeed engage in a flexible but conscious fitness program—often together. Part of most couples' time together is spent in tennis, golf, running, or swimming to maintain their physical fitness and stamina. Commuters determined to bring off the two-city situation need: jobs in two different cities (each too good to turn down); a tolerance for long hours on the airways or highways (with only the radio for company); immunity to earaches (from hours on the long-distance telephone); and an arsenal of energy.

Your Sense of Humor (Question 12). One more thing needs to be added to the list above if you're determined to bring off the commuter marriage—A FULL-TIME SENSE OF HUMOR. Under the glamorous facade of winging it across the country every week or so are the airline schedule foul-ups, the screaming infant in the seat behind you, the lost luggage, and countless other minor irritants that can leave you feeling downhearted. Besides problems with the traveling that is going to take a lot of your time off, there are the problems with your two residences. If one home seems to be in constant need of repair, with two you can count on dripping faucets, leaking sinks, stopped-up drains, and all the rest. Louise, a 32-year-old commuter from the Northwest reported how she planned a romantic honeymoon reunion with her husband Fred. It was late January and they hadn't been together since Christmas. She arranged the cognac and chocolate mints, candlelight and satin robe. What she couldn't arrange was the weather. Temperatures dropped to below zero, and when she and Fred returned from the airport, all the pipes in the house were frozen. They snatched up the cognac, chocolates, and satin robe and headed straight for the nicest hotel they could think of, where they spent the early part of the evening in a bubbling hot tub. "You have to roll with the punches," said Louise. "The secret is to be totally flexible, whatever comes. We just don't worry about it. We try to look at the humorous side of our unusual lifestyle and we especially never close the bedroom door on our sense of humor."

Managing Time (Question 13). Louise and Fred feel that flexibility is important, but the fact is, they organize their time rather rigidly. Their success as a commuter couple is dependent upon not allowing things like frozen water pipes to interfere with their time. They had set aside the weekend as their time together, and nothing could interrupt that organization. Long-distance marriage is a balancing act. You have to balance a work role with a domestic, intimate relationship. In order to allow enough time for each, you have to consistently set thoughtful priorities. For example, next week you can work late if necessary because your wife will be out of town, but right now she's here, so the work can wait. Next week Louise will have to face the frozen water pipe difficulties, but right now it's time for her and Fred to be together.

When there are children, the need to organize time becomes much greater. A large number of women feel that it is possible to be a good wife, a good mother, and a good worker all at the same time, but that there is a lot of pressure. Contrary to general belief, it is not work that creates the pressure—it's parenthood. Along with the good news that husbands are taking a greater role in parenting comes the bad news that although attitudes about domestic chores have changed, behavior hasn't. Despite a decade of consciousness-raising, new role models, and diminishing emphasis on traditional male-female stereotypes, women say overwhelmingly they do most household chores themselves. A few mothers are satisfied with the way household chores are divided. But of mothers of older children feel confident that they could fix their own meals, and that all household tasks are not their responsibility. Commuter wives and mothers fall into the supermom trap less frequently than dual-career wives with a single residence. They simply don't have the time. The successful couples manage and balance time carefully. If your life's a chaos with one residence, a two-city existence could be a disaster.

Work Flexibility (Question 14). When asked about what helped most to make the commuter relationship a bell-ringer arrangment, a large number of commuters reported "being lucky enough to have a flexible schedule." It is estimated that about half of the commuter marriages are in the academic world where work schedules are flexible and jobs are very scarce. But the number is growing in business, politics, journalism, publishing, and show business. Flexible work schedules could greatly increase the desirability of long-distance marriage. The thing that becomes clear in talking with couples is that there must be some flexibility—ideally flexibility for both partners. When a domestic crisis arises, it must be possible to arrange work to deal with it, since neither spouse has a domestic backup. As commuters say, "We both need a wife."

Beyond that, however, is the need to travel, and the frequency of contact with a spouse is important. If work can be compressed into even four instead of five days, intimacy time can be increased. Many of the successful commuters interviewed were those with their own businesses. They could arrange their own schedules, working long hours when needed and slacking off when requirements were less. Others were in sales or real estate, or were artists, writers, or architects. With increased distance between the two cities in which couples reside, flexibility of work schedules becomes even more important. When more money is required for travel, trips cannot be as frequent, so staying longer is necessary. "Banking" of off-duty time then becomes more important because the banked time can be used for added time with a family. If you have to punch a time clock or work a strictly five-day week on a 9-to-5 schedule, the logistics of your commuter marriage will be much more difficult. If *both* of you work the traditional work week, be prepared for some stressful times—or better, request a schedule change from your employers. It can be part of spouse bargaining. You might be surprised and find your company sympathetic, especially if, when you request the new schedule, you can give three solid reasons why it will benefit the organization.

Delegation of Tasks and Decision-Making (Questions 15, 16, 17). Do you feel you have to do everything yourself or else it either won't be done, or won't be done right? If you answered that you seldom or never delegate tasks at home or at work, you may be in trouble as a commuter. If you answered that you delegate every chance possible, you should do fine. Delegating responsibility is a part of management of your time and energy. In the commuting lifestyle there simply isn't time for you to do it all. Steel yourself to ignore nutritional needs for a time and let the children plan their own meals. They can even shop for the groceries and cook the dinners. It won't be pizza, hot dogs, hamburgers, and french fries forever. They'll decide they need something else (and besides, pizza is a very nutritious dish). It may or may not be true, but it's been said that an 8-year-old has the mental maturity for housekeeping; why not try it out? Do your schools serve hot lunches? If so, buy them. Are you (on top of everything else) the president of a service organization in your town? If so, let your vice president plan the year's meetings. How will the secretary in your office advance to an administrative position if not given responsibility? So it's not done exactly as you would have done it. Does it truly matter? Probably not. Save your energy for bigger things. What you need to concentrate on is problem-solving and decision-making. You'll have to do enormous amounts of problem-solving and decision-making in a commuter marriage. Besides, it gives you practice for when you become the chief executive officer of your company. The more you enjoy decision-making, the happier you'll be in a two-city marriage. The problem-solving in arranging time, money, recreation, travel becomes a real challenge. How many airline schedules can you keep in long-term memory? The more the better.

Leisure Interest in Common (Question 18). Profiles of grand slam commuter marriages show that although spouses are individualistic in many ways, they enjoy similar hobbies and sports activities. Reading, music, drama, fishing, hunting, golfing, tennis, bridge: the list of possibilities is endless. The ideal is at least two common leisure interests. Frequently couples develop their commuter lifestyles around these leisure interests. Remember the couple with the his-and-hers condos, both on golf courses. How about the well-to-do commuters who during their time together indulged their hobbies of skin-diving in the Bahamas and flying their private plane. Some of the less well-to-do report picnicking in nearby woods. The botanist couple worked in their garden. To keep a long-distance relationship strong there have to be common interests, and perhaps surprisingly, these common interests tend to deepen rather than to burn out, as seems too often to be the case with single-residence couples. Couples who live together full time frequently seek leisure activities with outsiders—as a type of release from overdoses of intimacy in a marriage. Commuters, on the other hand, continue their leisure activities together. Interdependence promotes effectiveness on the job, but it also promotes effectiveness in the intimate relationship. The strong relationship of commuter couples allows them to enjoy each other's company in leisure activities. It may be that this mutual enjoyment of leisure and sports creates a firm foundation that allows the couple to survive in the face of great storms of social disapproval from outsiders.

The Opinions and Attitudes of Others (Question 19). The social disapproval caused by the departure of commuter couples from traditional family norms and from breaking the unwritten marriage contract that gives the husband the right to decide how and where the couple will live is seen by most sociologists and psychologists as the most difficult problem the commuter couple has to face. Money and time difficulties can be annoying and cause frustration, but the Hester Prynne response to women commuters and the unmacho image attached to male commuters causes strains within the relationship. Even though most working couples are beginning to feel less guilty about their lifestyles as women approach 60 percent of the work force, the commuter couple is still a pariah. If you are bothered by the opinions of others, relatives and friends, be prepared to counteract the disapproval with ammunition about the large number of such marriages, the relatively low divorce rate, the high fidelity rate, and other information that can change the attitudes of these people who are important to you. Make sure that children and parents understand the situation—that you are *not* in the initial stage of marital breakdown.

A situation that may take more time to change is the response of business organizations which are culturally accustomed to the single-career two-person employee. Organizations were benefited by the unpaid services of the supportive spouse, and now they must begin to understand that although a trailing spouse may not be following, you are a valuable employee with high commitment to your career and to the company. Business organizations need to understand that by transferring women they won't be damaging marriages. At some companies women are considered a "transfer risk," but other companies are taking the risk and even sending women to overseas posts. If you need plenty of approval from others in order to bolster your self-image, a long-distance marriage could be stressful. If you're immune to the responses of others, or at least not quite so likely to break out in a rash at the raised eyebrow, you'll do fine. If you're a true loner, you'll have no problem at all.

Loneliness (Question 20). If you find you'd be mad as a hornet if you had to spend your birthday alone, you may find commuter marriage to be a difficult lifestyle. Loneliness is one of the most common complaints of commuter couples. They miss the daily sharing of experiences, not only big things, but the trivia of routine daily occurrences. And in a commuting situation, regardless of the planning, things can go wrong. With high commitment to a job, last-minute emergencies can arise that interrupt weekend plans. With uncertain airline schedules and equipment delays, you may not get there before the epicurean soufflé falls and some of the shine is off the romantic evening. You need plenty of flexibility and a sense of humor to weather these dangers to the relationship. You also need to be extremely self-sufficient and self-confident so that you won't fall prey to the "poor little me, all by myself" syndrome. You have to leave the idea of silent nights and empty days behind you. Loneliness is not simply the lack of people in your life. You can be lonely in a crowd and lonely in a good solid single-residence marriage. Keep in mind that there are other forms of communication besides face-to-face interaction. The telephone is a wonderful invention—albeit increasingly expensive, but some large companies are implementing satellite communication that you might use. There are intimacies you can indulge in on the telephone that are impossible face to face. Letter writing is another means of exchanging intimacies. Over half of the commuters interviewed said they were doing more and more letter writing. Some wrote every day even though they talked on the telephone, and they still report that this in no way diminished the pleasure of their visits. Solitude in itself doesn't produce loneliness; it comes when expectations fail. If expectations are altered to realistic levels for your commuting lifestyle rather than the single-career single-residence lifestyles, solitude can become enjoyable or at least tolerable. When it makes its appearance, do something nice for yourself. Where have you always wanted to go on your birthday, but never had the chance? What would you like to do, what would you like to eat, what would you like to drink? Treat yourself like a star.

Infidelity (Question 21). "My husband was willing to allow me to have new sexual experiences," Miss Samuelson said. "He was liberated or wide open or thought it was sort of neat to see what would happen. . . . I wasn't so willing to have him fool around with other women," (Rule 1977:60). But she began seeing other men. At first she was uncomfortable; she felt married. Slowly that changed. Terry Samuelson and George Stransky, her gynecologist husband, were eventually divorced. Terry believes that they were apart too long. He was in Anchorage and she was in Houston. She believes too many things both good and bad happened and they were unable to applaud each other or support each other. They eventually felt they didn't know each other well, but they still believe that it could have worked, "if you're careful."

All evidence available indicates that infidelity among commuter couples is about half what it is in the traditional single-residence marriage. Although on the surface it would seem otherwise, the lifestyle simply doesn't lend itself to promiscuity. There may be long periods of separation when certainly a spouse would be unlikely to "get caught," but this is balanced—in fact, overbalanced—by other factors. The first of these is career commitment. Commuter couples love their jobs. They are good at their work and enjoy doing it. They spend long hours in pursuit of career goals rather than in pursuit of extramarital affairs. Second, they are highly committed to their intimate relationship. As our grandmothers used to say, "She's found Mr. Right," and so has he found his "Mrs." Much of the energy that's left after career pursuits is spent in traveling. There's simply not enough time left over for infidelity. Finally, and most important, there is the increased communication of commuter couples. They have to talk; they have to discuss beforehand their unconventional lifestyle. When a couple decides to live together, apart, they discuss whether or not they will include sexual freedom as a part of the arrangement. Most agree not to, but some feel their relationship is strong enough to survive it. The major thing is that they do talk about it—many single-residence couples never do. If there is already underlying conflict in the marriage, it will surface regardless of the couple's living arrangements.

Established Careers (Question 22). If both of you are just now beginning your careers with little or no previous work experience, you will find that a commuter marriage lifestyle may be somewhat more difficult to manage. What you may find is that you both need a "wife." Not merely for usual domestic housework support that a traditional wife offers, but more important for the emotional backup needed when a new and challenging position is in its initial stages. Men will be especially susceptible to this stress because they miss the right to have the one career that really counts. But wives in the beginning stages of a career also need ego support. Women have only recently begun to make progress in attaining management and executive positions in organizations. For them, the territory is all but uncharted. Entering the "good old boys' club" is not always easy. There are many games that mother never taught you, and a supportive spouse at your side can sometimes help by supplying the rules.

If one of you, especially the husband, has already established a strong professional identity, things go much more easily. You can avoid the pitfalls of career conflicts that can make you competitors when what you want to be is best friends. When a husband has an already established career, a wife can avoid the guilty feelings about her own ambition because she has already paid her dues. Husbands then have a sense of satisfaction in their wives' development.

When both spouses have established careers before beginning their commuter lifestyle, it might be speculated that difficulties could arise from the extreme sense of independence each might have. Surprisingly, this does not seem to be the case. Most couples interviewed who were well established in their careers before their long-distance relationship began seemed to thrive on the situation. They indicated that commuting enriched their intimate relationship and brought their sexual life to a honeymoon fervor.

Response of Employers (Question 23). If your employers have responded in a positive way to your need for encouragement in your commuting marriage, things are going to be much easier for you. The types of help they can give range from reimbursement for travel expenses, to use of leased telephone lines, to maybe only an understanding verbal response when you talk about your marriage rather than a response that implies your marriage must certainly be on the rocks. Just as with the often negative response of friends and relatives to commuter marriage, you'll have to be prepared to refute the idea that marital breakdown is the reason for your decision to live apart. It is possible to convince employers that there are indeed many advantages to hiring long-distance couples and supporting their relationship. As one business executive said, "Motivation is our greatest shortage," and commuter couples are among the most highly motivated people available. They have high commitment to both their jobs and their relationships. By responding with some support to the commuter situation of dual-career couples, employers gain career-motivated individuals who are willing to give work responsibilities and career advancement top priority. The compartmentalization of domestic and work environments is another positive factor for organizations. It allows a spouse to work late and schedule appointments at all hours without worrying about how the marital partner will react.

But what can you ask in return from your employers? Remember the first consideration has to be "what's best for the company"; so bargaining has to be done when the opportunity is right. A few important things that help would be: phone lines, a travel expense allowance, and probably most important, flexible work schedules. The higher up you move in your organization, the more likely you are to have these things automatically.

So, if for now your employers are nonresponsive to your situation, it won't last forever. You'll be moving up, and a higher economic level will make things easier. Everything indicates that there will be larger numbers of commuter relationships in the future. As this happens, even dinosaur organizations will have to take notice and respond.

Children (Questions 24, 25). The response of couples during interviews clearly points to increased stress if a commuter couple has children, and not surprisingly, the more children, the greater the stress. Not all these difficulties can be attributed solely to the commuting, however. Dual-career couples with the traditional single-residence pattern also find that children can increase tensions, and the new corporate dropouts seem to be young, talented, self-confident women who find that parenthood and career are overly taxing despite their best intentions. A university professor stated that couples who want both dual careers and children will never make it to the top of their professions. He believes that childless couples will have an easier time of it, but that they will also have to accept weekend commuting if transfer is crucial to career advancement.

Some couples report 8-year-olds going through periods of depression, and some parents feel they are slowly but surely being cut out of the family group and replaced by others. When Marsha's daughter Roxanne no longer asked her mother to braid her hair when she was home on weekends and said instead "Daddy's going to do it," Marsha began to have regrets about accepting the opportunity in public relations that she had grabbed by moving to Chicago. Nevertheless, some couples do quite well with children in a long-distance marriage and believe that the quality time they spend together is more important than the quantity of togetherness. A lot seems to depend on how the couple feels. If they have a strong vision of equality and a powerful desire to make the situation work, the effect on children certainly need not be the negative one that some sociologists would like to propose. It seems ridiculous to suggest that children have less chance to "be normal" in a commuting arrangement when we have no tried and true method of child raising. Certainly in the male-dominated, traveling salesman type of long-distance marriage little was said about negative effects on children.

As seems logical, the older the children, the easier it is for commuter couples to adjust to living together, apart. But regardless of age, children need to understand why you have chosen this lifestyle. Most especially they need to understand that it is for something important to both of you—your career motivation. They need to understand that the marriage is a strong one and that the separation is not simply the first step toward divorce. With more women firmly established in careers, commuter marriage will be on the increase. This will make understanding of the relationship easier. Keep in mind too that children raised in a certain situation tend to think of it as the norm. In the Southwest, Hispanic children have peanut butter on corn tortillas for an afterschool snack, and they believe everyone does. Commuter children probably believe everyone lives in two cities. They don't realize that there is anything particularly exotic about what their family is doing.

A Commuter Marriage Model

A composite of ingredients for successful long-distance marriage would have to include: flexibility, common interests, interdependence, and a desire for self-actualization. The last, self-actualization, cannot be overemphasized. Women still feel gratitude when their husbands "allow" them to pursue their own careers, which implies that the American "macho" belief is seldom very far below the surface of most people's thinking. To allow a wife to pursue career activities that can result in higher pay than the male receives can be a tremendous threat to men. The existence of career competition within the family can also be a threat and can negate the possibility of self-actualization for both partners.

Commuter couples are indeed diverse, but if we should chose a typical generalized profile it would include the following:

- from 35 to 60 (having been employed continuously for 12 to 35 years);
- highly successful in their careers;
- upper-middle with combined income usually over $50,000 (often she makes the higher income);
- many in a second marriage that has lasted for over five years;
- parents of three children or fewer, who are usually grown;
- self-confident, self-reliant, well-dressed;
- physically fit;
- individualistic while enjoying similar hobbies.

Commuter marriage, women's new high-level career aspirations, and men's new involvement in parenting are not damaging the family. What is happening is that a new social structure is being developed. It is part of a much broader social revolution that will bring dramatic changes in business policy, the way we live, and the way we work. In this social revolution brought about by the full participation of women in the work force, there are two heads-of-household. Both pursue careers and at the same time maintain a family life together. In truth, the social revolution is now being lived by hundreds of thousands. It is outpacing the sociologists and psychologists, who should have been in the forefront suggesting ways of living with the dual-career structure. The commuter lifestyle is a complication of the larger dual-career situation, and this book has explored and elaborated psychological, sexual, social, business, and financial developments affecting commuter couples. It has also suggested what commuter couples can do to live with the new situation.

By way of summary, the profiles below of people in successful dual-career, dual-residence marriages present a composite of ingredients necessary for success.

Myra and John. Born between the two world wars, Myra and John fell in love and were married in the late 1940s. They were in their early 20s, and John had begun to study for his baccalaureate degree in order to take advantage of the G. I. Bill. Myra already had her degree and was teaching elementary school. They were by no means well off financially. After five years John was working in personnel management, and they had two children, a boy and a girl—just as they had planned. At age 35, John went back to school and got an MBA and in time became a successful management consultant. Myra returned to school when the children were in junior high, and over a period of time earned her doctorate in education. She became highly renowned in her specialty and was soon writing texts and working on research sponsored by the National Institute of Education. Myra and John collaborated on books, but eventually the inevitable for dual-career marriage occurred. Myra was offered a very attractive and lucrative position at a university 1,000 miles away, and she left home. By this time the children were grown and on their own, but it was still not easy for the couple to split up and for Myra to move away from the city in which they had lived for twenty-two years. The lucky part was that they had plenty of flexibility in their work schedules as well as high income; so they were able to travel each weekend unless business and work commitments reduced their time together. They always kept at least two weekends a month exclusively for each other. Myra and John have continued this commuter style of marriage for twelve years. They spend prolonged vacations together and don't plan on a permanent retirement. When describing their relationship and their lifestyles, they say, "We have the best."

Betty and Robert. Married in the late sixties, Betty and Robert are considerably younger than Myra and John. They have three children who were born over a period of ten years, so there are two teenagers at home and one child now in college. Both Betty and Robert had only their baccalaureate degrees when they were married in California. They were activists in the peace movement and eventually returned to school and received masters and doctorate degrees in educational administration. After graduation, while he remained in a top administrative post in public education, she became a private consultant to business. She was soon offered a position with a multinational corporation 500 miles away from their home. Both Robert and Betty were convinced that it was a move worth making—the sort of opportunity that comes "once in a lifetime." Betty moved and took the youngest child with her. The two older children remained with Robert. They continued their commuter lifestyle for three years and are now back together. Both partners think the back-and-forth weekend visits had a positive effect on their marriage. Robert says, "I sure found out how dependent we were on the traditional parent role models. I learned an enormous amount. It gave me new opportunities, new knowledge and new skills. We appreciate each other." Betty responds, "It made an already successful marriage even greater."

References

Barrett, Karen. 1984. "Two-Career Couples: How They Do It." Ms. (June), p. 39.

Berger, P. and H. Keller. 1964. "Marriage and the Construction of Reality." Diogenes, 64:1–23.

Bird, Caroline. 1979. The Two-Paycheck Marriage. New York: Rawson Wade.

Blumstein, Philip and Pepper Schwartz. 1983. American Couples: Money, Work, Sex. New York: William Morrow.

Borders, William. 1980. "Away-on-Work Husbands and Marital Strains." New York Times, November 10.

Brown, Barbara A., Ann E. Freedman, Harriet N. Katz, and Alice M. Price. 1977. Women's Rights and the Law: The Impact of the ERA on State Laws. New York: Praeger.

Business Week. 1978. "Commuting: A Solution for Two-Career Couples." (April 3), pp. 65–68.

Cecere, Linda. 1983. "The Loneliness of the Long-Distance Marriage." Working Woman (October), pp. 136–39.

Crawford, Mary. 1979. "Two Careers, Three Kids, and Her 2,000 Mile Commute." Ms. (August), pp. 76–78.

Delatiner, Barbara. 1981. "Whither Thou Goest—Thou Goest." Working Mother (March), p. 87.

Dexter, Ed. 1977. "Marriage Without Proximity." Marriage, Divorce and Family Newsletter (April), p. 6.

Farris, Agnes. 1978. "Commuting." In Rhonda Rapoport and Robert Rapoport with Janice M. Bumstead, eds., Working Couples, pp. 100–7. New York: Harper and Row.

Flynn, W. Randolph and Judith U. Litzsinger. 1981. "Careers Without Conflict." Personnel Administrator (July), p. 81.

Fogarty, Michael P., Rhonda Rapoport, and Robert Rapoport. 1971. Sex, Career, and Family. London: Allen and Unwin.

Friedman, Dick. 1981. "Where His Career Leads Would You Follow?" Working Woman (June), pp. 15–18.

Gallese, Liz Roman. 1978. "Moving Experiences: Women Managers Say Job Transfers Present a Growing Dilemma." *Wall Street Journal* (May 4), p. 1.

Gaylin, Judy. 1983. "How Supermoms Can Cope." *Family Weekly* (October 9), p. 19.

Gerstel, Naomi and Harriet Gross. 1984. *Commuter Marriage: A Study of Work and Family.* New York: Guilford Press.

Getschow, George. 1980. "A Tale of Two Cities Has an Unhappy End for Some Executives." *Wall Street Journal* (February 1), p. 1.

Goodrick, Evelyn. 1980. "Making a Commuter Marriage Work." *McCall's* (July), p. 68.

Gottschalk, Earl C. 1983. "Trendy Dwellings: The 'Affordable' Home Turns Out to Be Tiny and Not Really Cheap." *Wall Street Journal* (December 7), p. 1.

Gross, Harriet Engel. 1980. "Dual-Career Couples Who Live Apart: Two Types." *Journal of Marriage and the Family* (August), pp. 567–76.

Grossman, Allyson Sherman. 1981. "The Employment Situation for Military Wives." *Monthly Labor Review* (February), pp. 60–64.

Hagen, Mary. 1980. "Yvonne Weber, Wildlife Biologist." *Colorado Woman* (October), p. 45.

Handy, Charles. 1978. "Going Against the Grain: Working Couples and Greedy Occupations." In Rhonda Rapoport and Robert Rapoport with Janice M. Bumstead, eds., *Working Couples*, pp. 36–46. New York: Harper and Row.

Henderson, Lana. 1979. "Career vs. Family." *Texas Woman* (May), pp. 19–25.

Hite, Shere. 1976. *The Hite Report.* New York: Macmillan.

Hogan, Patricia. 1980. "Career Women and Changing Lifestyles." *Executive Female* (July–August), pp. 34–38.

Hughston, George and Terri Eisler. 1984. "Commuter Marriage Challenge Inspires Survival Manual." *Research News: Arizona State University* (March), pp. 6–7.

Hunter, Bill. 1982. "On the Job Relocation." *Working Woman* (February), pp. 16–18.

Kaplan, Janice. 1979. "He/She." *Self* (March), pp. 38–41.

Kirschner, Betty Frankle and Laurel Richardson Walum. 1978. "Two-Location Families." *Alternative Lifestyles* (November), pp. 513–26.

Langley, Monica. 1981. "Some U.S. Jobs Turn Strong Marriages into Weekend Ones." *Wall Street Journal* (August 18), p. 1.

Lavoie, Rachel. 1977. "The Loneliness of the Long-Distance Marriage." *Money* (August), pp. 76–87.

Leo, John. 1982. "Marital Tales of Two Cities." *Time* (January 25), pp. 83–84.

McMurty, Larry. 1983. "Silent Nights, Empty Days: Leaving Loneliness Behind." *Family Weekly* (December 11), p. 4.

Maples, Mary F. 1981. "Dual Career Marriages: Elements for Potential Success." *The Personnel and Guidance Journal* (September), pp. 19–23.

Maynard, Cathleen E. and Robert A. Zawacki. 1979. "Organizations Must Meet This Challenge: Is Yours Ready?" *Personnel Journal* (July), pp. 469–72.

Nichols, William C. 1978. "Long-Distance Marriage." *Parents' Magazine* (October), p. 54.

O'Brien, Patricia. 1979. "Will Husbands Play Second Fiddle to Executive Wives?" *Miami Herald* (June 5), p. 1C.

O'Toole, Patricia. 1982. "Moving Ahead by Moving Around." *Savvy* (April), pp. 37–41.

Perry, Elisabeth I. 1983. "The Unhappy Lot of the Academic Couple with Two Careers and One Job." *The Chronicle of Higher Education* (September 14), p 64.

Rapoport, Rhonda, Robert N. Rapoport, and Ziona Strelitz with Stephen Kew. 1977. *Father, Mothers, and Society*. New York: Basic Books.

Rhodes, Jewell Parker and Edwardo Lao Rhodes. 1984. "Commuter Marriage the Toughest Alternative." *Ms.* (June), p. 44.

Riechers, Maggie. 1978. "When You Both Work." *Women's Work* (May–June), p. 5.

Rossi, Alice. 1964. "Equality Between the Sexes: An Immodest Proposal." *Daedalus*, 93(2):607–52.

_____ 1968. "Transition to Parenthood." *Journal of Marriage and the Family*, 30(1):26–39.

Rule, Sheila. 1977. "Long-distance Marriage on the Rise." *New York Times* (October 31), p. 33.

Savvy. 1983. "Twenty at the Top." (April), pp. 38–47.

Schneider, D. M. 1978. *American Kinship: A Cultural Account*. Englewood Cliffs, N.J.: Prentice-Hall.

Seixas, Suzanne. 1981. "Marriage as a Fortnightly Affair." *Money* (May), p. 78.

Toman, Barbara. 1983. "Parenthood and Career Overtax Some Women Despite Best Intentions." *Wall Street Journal* (September 7), p. 1.

U.S. *News and World Report*. 1977. "Commuter Marriages: Latest Product of Women's Changing Status." (October 24), pp. 109–10.

Van Hulsteyn, Peggy. 1977. "Why Those Commuting Marriages Aren't What They're Cracked Up to Be." *Mademoiselle* (September), pp. 84–86.

Index

Author's Note

As this book goes to press, a new support network for commuter couples and families is being organized. For further information, send a stamped, self-addressed envelope to:

Commuter Couples Association of America
1109 South Plaza Way, #242
Flagstaff, AZ 86001